THE WIND AT THE DOOR

The Wind at the Door

Maggie Durran

CELEBRATION

KINGSWAY PUBLICATIONS
EASTBOURNE

First published 1986

ISBN 0 86065 412 5

The text of 'They Cast Their Nets in Galilee' by William A. Percy is used by permission.

Front cover photo shows the Cathedral of the Isles on Cumbrae

Published in the USA by Celebration,
P.O. Box 309, Aliquippa, Pennsylvania 15001, USA.

Printed in Great Britain for
KINGSWAY PUBLICATIONS LTD
Lottbridge Drove, Eastbourne, E. Sussex BN23 6NT by
Cox & Wyman Ltd, Reading.
Typeset by Nuprint Services Ltd, Harpenden, Herts AL5 4SE.

Contents

Acknowledgements

From the first glimmer of the idea for this book Steven Plummer of the Community of Celebration helped with interviews, typing and editing and offered constant encouragement. Thank you.

Many thanks to all the past and present members of the Community of Celebration in Millport, who gave their time to be interviewed.

Special thanks to those people from Millport who have known and befriended the Community, who told of their experience of sharing their life with the Community for a very significant ten years.

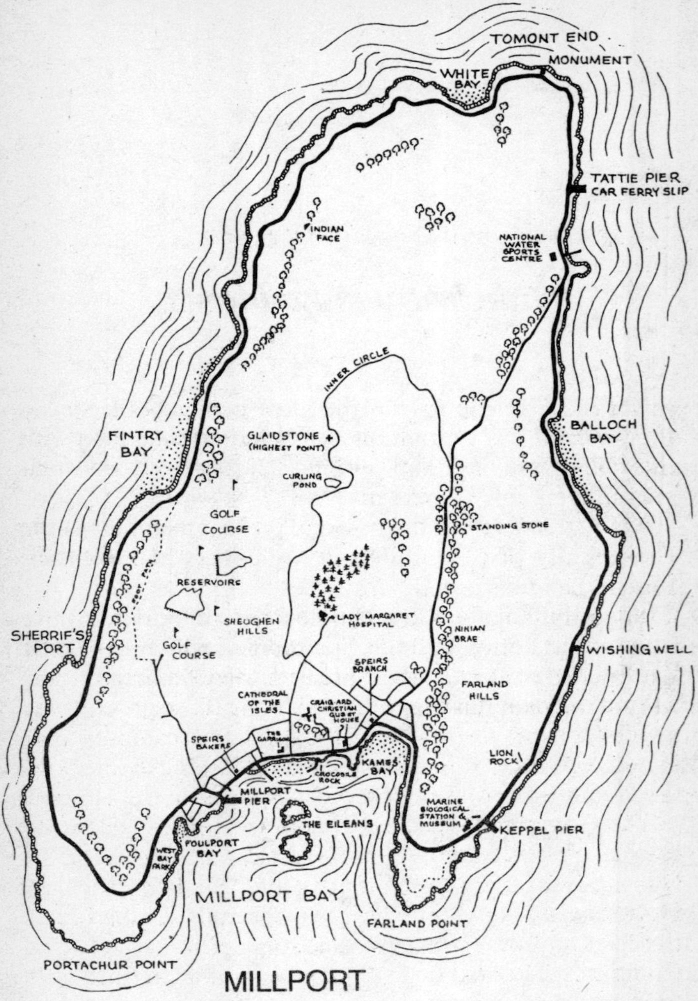

THE ISLE OF CUMBRAE

CHAPTER ONE

Finding a New Home

In 1973 the group left Coventry and took occupancy of a disused convent property in Berkshire—near the village of Wargrave—a property then owned by the monks of Nashdom Abbey. There the community assumed an official name: The Community of Celebration.

Newsletter July 1980

Graham Pulkingham and Bill Farra were away from the Community to undertake a weekend's ministry at Old St Paul's Church in Edinburgh. The ministry was fruitful and a time of growth for the church. Among those present was a missioner in the Episcopal Church; he came up and introduced himself to Graham and Bill asking them about the Community of Celebration back home in Berkshire.

The Community of Celebration was conscious that its lease at Yeldall Manor, near Reading, was short-term. So Bill and Graham were fairly interested in Richard Holloway's next words: 'Have you seen the Cathedral of the Isles and the College of the Holy Spirit on the Isle of Cumbrae?' He went on to explain that it was an Episcopal foundation without an Episcopal ministry. In fact, the Bishop was looking for a means of re-establishing a ministry at the Cathedral.

It was an interesting idea, no more. However, Bill and Graham decided to go home via the Isle of Cumbrae. Once on the island, they found a quiet town, isolated from mainland life, and the Cathedral, sitting on a hill overlooking the town. The property consisted of a tiny cathedral that could seat about a hundred people. The tall spire was visible above the trees that surrounded the terraced slopes around it. Joined to the cathedral at the east end and running south was South College, a long narrow building with a cloister, two large reception rooms on the ground floor and a row of little cell-like bedrooms on the first floor, each named after a saint. Across a narrow cinder path from South College was an Annexe, a post-war, prefabricated building whose architecture clashed awkwardly with that of the Cathedral buildings. The cloister of South College turned a right angle east next to the refectory and brought them out on a pavement, past the east end of the Lady Chapel, to North College. This, like the Annexe, was detached from the Cathedral building, but was barely six feet from the corner of the Lady Chapel. The North College was built to accommodate students; the ground floor had two large reception rooms and several small bedrooms. On the first floor more tiny rooms opened on each side of the central hallway that ran the length of the building. North College looked west, its sitting room giving a good view of the blank north wall of the Lady Chapel and Cathedral, but more particularly it had a clear view, across an orchard and vegetable garden, onto the hills, fields and woodland toward the heart of the island. Away to the west, over the spur of the hill was the Clyde and the Mull of Kintyre in the distance.

The two visitors shrugged as they left. The whole place was overgrown, damp and dilapidated. The path down to the main gate, once a wide approach like the gate through

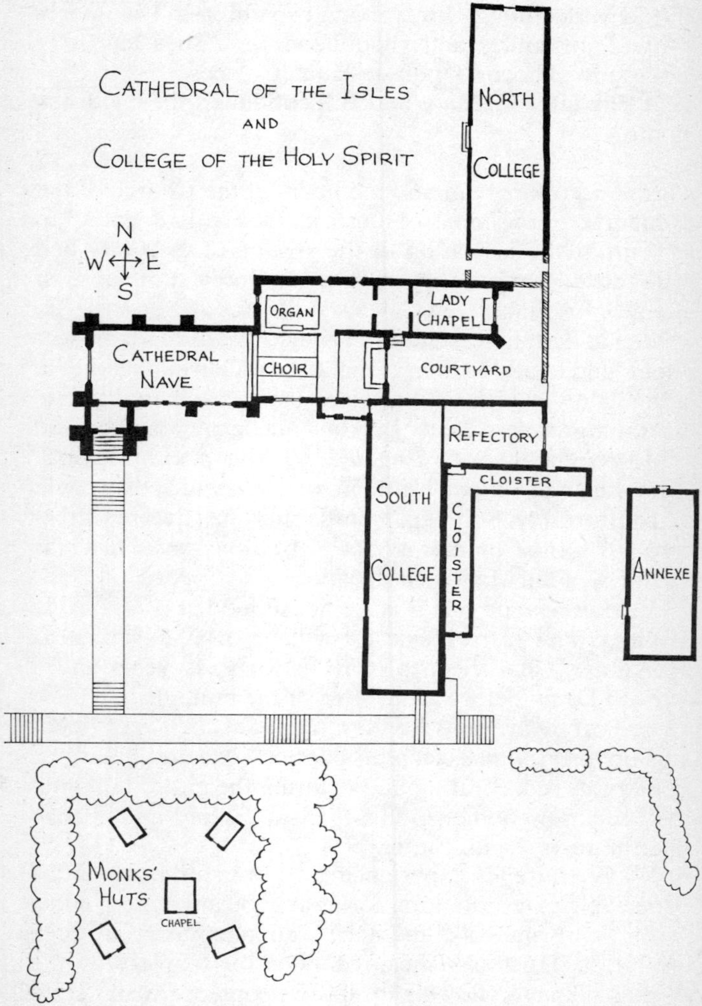
CATHEDRAL OF THE ISLES
AND
COLLEGE OF THE HOLY SPIRIT
N
W
E
S
NORTH
COLLEGE
ORGAN
LADY
CHAPEL
CATHEDRAL
NAVE
CHOIR
COURTYARD
REFECTORY
CLOISTER
SOUTH
COLLEGE
CLOISTER
ANNEXE
MONKS'
HUTS
CHAPEL

which a coach and horses could have passed, was now barely wide enough for walking two abreast. The undergrowth, brambles and rhododendron bushes had long since spread beyond their designated places.

A day later Graham and Bill continued their journey home.

Graham Pulkingham and members of the Church of the Redeemer Episcopal, Houston, Texas had come to Britain at the invitation of the Bishop of Coventry and had settled temporarily in Potter's Green. For those of the new Community in Coventry, life was often a struggle. Living in Britain was a major change of culture for most of them, and to add to their trauma, they all lived together in a bungalow, which though spacious was sadly inadequate for their numbers. Betty Pulkingham began praying. God had brought them to England, so what was he saying? Surely he had a home for them, one into which they could fit comfortably. Some six months later, just before Christmas 1973, the Community of Celebration moved to a new home, Yeldall Manor, in the Diocese of Oxford.

Yeldall Manor was a large house hidden down a tiny country lane just outside the village of Wargrave near Reading. It had been a convent for forty years and a private home before that. Most of the building had been closed off by the nuns, so the Community began by opening up the rooms, cleaning out the soot and cobwebs, repairing, redecorating and rewiring the entire building. At their new home, God began to expand and change their ministry significantly.

Many churches experiencing a powerful move of the Holy Spirit were looking for help and came into contact with the Fisherfolk and Celebration ministry through Fountain Trust. As the invitations for ministry by the Fisherfolk came flowing in, more people were invited to come from the United States to join the expanding teams. The Fisherfolk became two, then three teams to meet the variety of invitations. Within fairly easy reach of London and the motorways, Yeldall was ideally located for the travelling ministry. It was also easy for hosts of visitors to find. Soon large numbers were joining the Community for its weekly Eucharist and for its evening of prayer and praise, and many of them joined the Community family. It was a place of excitement, a focus for renewal and worship.

It was at Yeldall Manor that Betty Pulkingham and Mimi Farra worked with Jeanne Harper on the music for the songbook *Sound of Living Waters*. Their office had once been the sitting room of the convent's mother superior. Now it was filled almost to overflowing with old furniture collected from all over the house. Someone had cleared just enough space for Betty to have a piano and one stool, with access to it through a wall of furniture on either side. Many of the rooms were in similar or worse condition, but gradually the Community were able to clear and clean enough rooms to make life and work fairly reasonable.

In the hub-bub of this busy house it was not so easy to recognize the deep things the Spirit was working among the Community. On the surface there was the highly effective travelling ministry of the Fisherfolk teams. There was healing and pastoral care that was changing many lives; and there was training for church leaders who came and lived among the Community to learn from their life.

Within two years of the Community's arrival at Yeldall it was apparent to the trustees of the property that the time was right to sell the house. There were many conversations within the Community. Perhaps it would be possible for them to buy the house and continue to live there? Perhaps the funds could be raised to make an offer? But God was to say something completely different to the Community.

It soon became apparent that the Community's growing numbers and escalating ministry in worship leadership made it necessary to consider a new home. There was a growing awareness that the Community should be more isolated, to allow a more considered and reflective approach to both life and ministry. They desired a place which was less exposed, where they would be able to develop their teachings, worship materials and make recordings; a place of retreat, perhaps a base from which they could continue their public ministry. They would need to hear God very clearly, unmistakably, for this move would help to shape and define the life and ministry of the Community. They were wanting to know what God was making of them.

Graham and Bill arrived home from Scotland to all these questions that had prompted them to take a look at the Scottish island. During the weekend a small group of Dutch people had stayed with the Community, to share in worship and experience their lifestyle. The Community was by then over a hundred people, working closely with the local parish; they had come from Britain, Canada, and more recently a family and a single man had come from Sweden. Another Swedish priest, Lisa Tegby, was about to arrive and a Swedish family that had met the Fisherfolk at a conference the previous summer was also soon to arrive. The Dutch group left after sharing a prophecy with the Community. Before they left Holland, the Lord had given them a prophecy that they were sure was not for their own group, so they shared it with others they met. That way it would be identified by those to whom the Lord was speaking. The prophecy stated that a renewal ministry would be established in a link between people from

London and Stockholm, to be located off the west coast of Scotland. Was this prophecy for the Community of Celebration?

Bill and Graham began to open the post that had accumulated in their absence. One letter was from a Presbyterian minister in the United States. This man had reached a very dry place in his ministry and had gone to a retreat centre in California for refreshment. The organized programme was no help, so the retreat master sent the minister off on his own to sit before the Lord and to wait till the Lord spoke to him. The minister chose to spend this time sitting in the shadow of a huge Celtic cross that looked out onto the Pacific Ocean. At last God spoke to him, a curious instruction. He heard the Lord clearly say that he should contact Graham Pulkingham in Largs. The minister knew of Graham and knew his address to be in Berkshire, but had no idea why Graham's name should be linked with the little town of Largs on the west coast of Scotland. Graham knew why—Largs was the town across the Clyde from Millport on the Isle of Cumbrae. It was from Largs that everyone caught the ferry to the island.

Bill and Graham's visit to the island, though seemingly uneventful did not go unnoticed. Within days of his return south to Yeldall Manor Graham received a phone call from the Bishop of Argyle and the Isles who wished to talk about the Cathedral of the Isles. Graham flew to Glasgow to talk with him.

The deed of trust of the Cathedral and College, now about a hundred years old, had been established as an Episcopal ministry and for post-ordination training in worship and liturgy. In Scotland, the Episcopal Church is not the established church like its counterpart, the Church of England. The established church in Scotland is the Presbyterian Church.

At the time resident on the Cathedral premises was a

small group from Youth with a Mission who lived in North College. The pastoral ministry was temporarily served by Roland Walls, a monk from the Community of the Transfiguration, at Roslin near Edinburgh. Roland spent part of each year in retreat on Cumbrae, living in a tiny hut in the Cathedral grounds. The Bishop was interested in establishing an Episcopal ministry in the Cathedral, with a priest resident there, and to make use of the buildings to further the aims and goals of the original trust. The Community of Celebration were constantly involved in ministry and teaching in the field of worship and liturgy, though not post-ordination training.

The Community reached the point of having to take seriously all the pointers that were being presented to them. Were these signs of God leading them to a new place, to the Isle of Cumbrae?

Graham and Bill described the tiny stone cathedral and its cold, stone colleges that could become their home. There were ferries regularly to the mainland and the town seemed fine, like any other small town. There was an attraction in the relationship the Community could have to the Cathedral and its congregation. The lease that the Bishop was offering was for all the premises, including the Cathedral, and the Community would serve, through one of its own priests, the needs of the parishioners. This was potentially an environment where the Community could be more at home in the church than at Yeldall Manor. Graham would be the Provost, but as long as there was an Episcopally ordained person to conduct services, he would be free to travel. There was more than one priest in the Community who could take such responsibility for the small Cathedral congregation.

The island was far enough off the beaten track, but was it too far? Would it be too isolated for Fisherfolk teams and Betty Pulkingham to get on with the work of ministry?

The buildings themselves seemed to offer space for the development of a Fisherfolk training programme. For some time now churches visited by the Fisherfolk teams had been asking for their own musicians to be trained in worship leadership. Perhaps in addition, there would be sufficient space to run occasional conferences.

Within the large Community at Yeldall Manor there were all sorts of people. Not only were there various nationalities but there were various different community callings. The group that gradually formed around the calling to the Isle of Cumbrae was one which was to see itself as a community within the church, identifiable and finding the focus and meaning of life in their fellowship together. Out of this fellowship and life they would serve the local neighbourhood as well as national and international ministries. Some members of the Community had come for a defined period of time to learn about and experience community life; these people would take this back to the churches from which they had come, not to form identical communities but to be the yeast in the flour, to share a quality of life with the rest of the church.

The ministry in the south was still very busy, with constant invitations coming from churches and conferences for teaching and worship leadership. The Community saw the need to divide its resources in order to maintain an active ministry presence in England. One of the Fisherfolk teams, with their families and the business which marketed the Community's worship resources, Celebration Services, would move to Post Green in Dorset to continue the work.

In the United States another small group was preparing to become a community. The Church of the Redeemer was forming a small community around its ministry business and that group had been invited by Bishop Frey of Colorado to establish themselves in his diocese, to be the Community of Celebration in the United States. Several members from Yeldall Manor went to join the Colorado community.

God had gathered these people from various churches and various countries to experience being his family together in a very particular way. The move to Cumbrae was the catalyst for scattering them once again throughout the world. However, they were still to be of one family. The 'society' of communities formed by this scattering were to stay in fellowship and commitment to one another, to help one another, to share financial resources and offer one another their skills and talents.

The local parish church near Yeldall Manor, Wargrave, had been doubled by the arrival of the Community of Celebration in 1973. Local people had been suspicious of the friendly hugs during the Peace, as well as the musical vivacity. But they came to be accepted as committed members of the congregation, a little different maybe, but with gifts in worship leadership that had added enormously to the church. The Community's departure would leave spaces, large ones, in the church's structure. Seeds had been sown, however, and eventually two Community families bought houses and continued to live in Wargrave.

In the small town of Millport, rumours began to spread. Some years before a group of American hippies had taken up residence in the Cathedral property. There were many suspicions about them at the time, confirmed at last when their leader was arrested on drug charges and the whole group dispersed. There were bad memories such as when the beautiful antique furniture had been damaged. Youth with a Mission had temporary residence on the College property, as did the organist for the Cathedral. Roland Walls made his occasional visits. The Bishop's plan to lease all the property to a community and so provide a full priestly ministry would change all these now comfortable arrangements. Some people in the town were sure they would not like such a group—also mostly American—to come among them. There was considerable resistance.

CHAPTER TWO

'And the Strength of the Hills is His Also'

On December 1st the Fisherfolk Training Programme shared in the Diocesan Missionary Eucharist at the Glasgow Cathedral of St. Mary the Virgin, with the Bishop of Glasgow celebrating and Graham preaching. We sang the Melchizedek setting, including the new 'Scottish Gloria' which Betty Jane wrote. This is an arrangement for the organ that includes sounds of bagpipes.

Newsletter 9th December 1975

Cathleen and Bob Morris were in the United States with their four-month-old daughter Clare, when they received a telephone call from Yeldall. Would they consider being the first Community members to go to Millport? Bob could begin to be the priest to the Cathedral congregation and other members of the Community would join them later.

The Morrises cut short their holiday by a week and arrived in Wargrave to pack their belongings. Two days later with the baby still in jet-lag, they caught the overnight train to Glasgow. With them went Jackie Kemp, a single woman who had lived at Yeldall Manor for a year.

Some eighteen hours later, after a blustery ferry crossing from Largs, the bus dropped them in College Street which was the only address they had for the Cathedral. The sky was grey and the old stone buildings bleak. They looked around for a means of getting up the hill to the Cathedral.

'Oh no,' muttered Jackie. 'We've been sent here to die!'

A GPO repairman took pity on them standing there on the pavement with all their belongings in cases and boxes lying around their feet. 'Jump in the van. I'll take you up the hill,' he said.

North College was at that time divided in half: part was still inhabited by Youth with a Mission; the other was to be their home. Earlier that week several people had visited to clear and clean. Two rooms were available, one for the Morrises and one for Jackie.

There was no heating, and though the fireplace looked promising, there was no coal anywhere to be found. Besides, none of them had ever lit a coal fire before, and would not know how to go about it even if there had been coal to light.

A couple of them trudged back down the hill to buy food and essentials to last till Monday only to find that on a normal winter's Saturday afternoon most of the shops were closed.

Late that night Bob and Jackie, who was to be the new organist, stumbled into the Cathedral to prepare for the following morning's Eucharist. The Sunday morning service proved to be a drastic change. After the warmth and fellowship of the Wargrave Parish Church, the Cathedral was to them cold and uninviting. There were thirty-two people present, though to the newcomers it felt extremely sparse. The traditional Scottish liturgy felt heavy, and Bob found it difficult to celebrate the Eucharist at the high altar with his back to the congregation.

It would not be long before others would arrive from

the south, so Bob and Cathleen and Jackie spent most if not all of their time preparing more rooms in North and South colleges for their arrival.

Some years before, in Houston, Betty Pulkingham had been impressed by some hymn words and wrote an anthem called 'The Fishermen'.

They cast their nets in Galilee
Just off the hills of brown;
Such happy, simple fisherfolk,
Before the Lord came down.

Contented, peaceful fishermen,
Before they ever knew
The peace of God that filled their hearts
Brimful, and broke them too.

Young John who trimmed the flapping sail,
Homeless, in Patmos died.
Peter, who hauled the teeming net,
Head-down was crucified.

The peace of God, it is no peace,
But strife closed in the sod.
Yet, brothers, pray for but one thing:
The marvellous peace of God.

Words by William A. Percy

It was only later that the travelling team realized, 'Look, we wrote about ourselves even before we had a name.' Now, as Betty waited on the quay at Largs for the ferry, the breaking waves on the shore brought back the haunting introduction to the song. It seemed to have been written for this place. The song spoke of both Jesus and the disciples being broken by God. She had experienced brokenness in the Community; hearts broken from their hardness, to die to the world. For Betty music often reflected God's voice.

For all the Community, worship had become the heart and focus of life. When they came together, life was lived in a way that was more than just the adding together of individual gifts. God added an ingredient of corporate life that brought growth to individuals. The Holy Spirit working among them broke down the barriers that hampered life and worked miracles in their midst.

For Betty the sea breaking on the rocky shores of the Clyde and the harsh weather stripped away the protectiveness of modern culture and brought new meaning to the words '... and the strength of the hills is his also.'

Those Scottish rocks, among the oldest mountain ranges in the world, brought a sense of God that Betty could drink in, a richness and a sense of heritage of the Celtic church and its sense of God through many generations.

The Church of the Redeemer sent a representative to Graham's installation as Provost of the Cathedral of the Isles and the College of the Holy Spirit. Gordon Abbott stayed in a guest house in Kames Bay. He had never, as a native of Houston, experienced anything like the weather in Scotland. As he had driven north from the airport, the weather got heavier and gloomier, cold and misty. He found the unheated house amazing; it was like moving to a different planet.

On Friday 7th March, Graham was installed as Provost. It was a sung Eucharist at which the Bishop of Argyle and the Isles presided. Graham preached from readings about the Holy Spirit in Acts and John's gospel. Betty and the Fisherfolk led the music. The congregation that day were mostly newcomers from the Community of Celebration, but others came from the island to see who the new people were and, hesitantly, to welcome their arrival.

With the help of a local vicar who came regularly to the weekly praise and teaching evening the Community at Yeldall had bought an old green coach. To have paid removal costs for all the people moving north would have been exorbitant, and the coach provided an alternative. The long back seat was left in place, as were two or three seats near the front. All the seats in between were stripped out. The mechanic, who was essential to the well-being of this elderly and often sensitive vehicle, was Hokan, a Swedish priest, whose family was among the next to move to Cumbrae. The old bus made many trips to and from Cumbrae carrying people, boxes and furniture as well as a number of pens of chickens till by July most people were moved.

There was only a small ferry servicing the island in those days, which could carry only a handful of cars. Taking the coach across the Clyde was a chore. Not only did it leave no room for other vehicles, but the men on the ferry had to manoeuvre long planks of wood into position to enable the coach to get up or down the steep slip on the island. They didn't always want to. A piece of metal ripped from the back of the coach on one such attempt. On one of the final runs the coach nearly slipped into the Clyde.

The coach was retired, parked carefully behind North College to become Betty Pulkingham and Mimi Farra's music office for the preparation of the songbook *Fresh Sounds*.

Living in England had not prepared the Community for life in Scotland. Those from other parts of the world who had thought Britain was so small that it would be the same all over had quite a shock. There were immediate attempts to improve both buildings and grounds. Most rooms had no heating other than tiny coal fires and the wind whistled in at the doors and windows. They struggled with tons of coke and their van broke down; they then had to bring it up the steep hill in wheelbarrow loads. The fight against the elements and the struggle for survival certainly brought home the reality of living in Scotland!

Phil Higgs arrived from Chorleywood, in the rich and comfortable south of England, to join the Fisherfolk training programme that was about to begin. He drove up in a small Fiat that he owned. It was a beautiful day, clear, crisp and warm. The air was fresh and he found many members of the Community out clearing the grounds, opening a path from the main gate up to the Cathedral. Each day the Fisherfolk trainees spent the afternoons on maintenance, cutting back undergrowth and repairing buildings, including reconstruction of all the sewer drainage from North College.

Val Nobbs was also originally from the south of England. She had never realized the tension between England and Scotland. The English are proud of themselves, but here in Scotland to be identified as English was to be labelled an oppressor. Comments such as, 'Oh, you're a Sassenach, are you!' were not particularly friendly.

The International Fisherfolk Team had been in the United States on tour. It was time to come to Scotland, though they had not seen the island yet. They arrived in December in the midst of gales and for two weeks, until their rooms were ready in North College, they stayed in 'bed and breakfast' accommodation. It was housing designed for summer tourists, not for keeping people warm through winter storms when the waves splashed up against the bedroom windows of the houses on the sea front. In the States and even at Yeldall there had been warmth and colour, but here the dark greyness of the stone buildings and the dreary wet weather were depressing. It was hard not to complain. Laundry facilities were limited, two people working each day to do the laundry of a large household. Since there were several babies in nappies, these got priority. Everyone else was encouraged to be careful about how much laundry they created; not changing clothes too often. The hot water supply was limited and the boiler temperamental. 'Bath days' as well as 'laundry days' were instituted. There were reminiscences of times when you could have a bath whenever you wanted! Ice formed inside the windows and the little coke fires blew out if the wind was in the wrong direction. There was no central heating or air conditioning dial to set.

The Community family was in the intense process of building their new life. There was not a great deal of money for the common purse, so in addition to ministry, there was all kinds of work to keep life going. There were work days and expeditions to pick blackberries, harvest apples, make jam, wine, cider, and pies for the freezer. The kitchen in South College which served all the households was crammed with people. The grounds began to look more orderly and visitors joined the work. Often so many people were working, it was nearly impossible to organize everyone's comings and goings and meals. They muddled along for a while.

Late one afternoon Graham and Cathleen were working in the kitchen. Graham was making mayonnaise. Inadvertently, the lid was left off the blender and the whole kitchen was sprayed with mayonnaise. They exploded with laughter, cleaned up the mess and started again. But they made the same mistake—again!

Barbara Gilbert moved from Wargrave after giving up her teaching post. She was used to commuter traffic, people jumping into their cars, fighting the traffic and the lights to get to work. She walked up the tree-lined quietness of Cow Lane and into her office to do accounts. The sea was so close, its sound endlessly changing and endlessly the same, and yet always there. Harsh as it was at times, for her Cumbrae would become more of a home than she had ever known previously.

The Scottish education proved very different and often more difficult than the English. It seemed that Scottish teachers worked to harden up their children, to prepare them for the harsh reality of adult life.

Gordon Abbott had gone home from the installation service both cold and damp, yet still had heard God speak to him of his family joining the Community on Cumbrae. Susan was a little surprised, but not a lot, for God had already spoken to her about moving to Britain. The Community purchased a house in George Street. The garden of the house backed onto the Cathedral property down a narrow path near the Monks' Huts. The house was cleaned and redecorated, the mould was cleaned off, and all it lacked was a proper kitchen. After the Abbotts moved into the George Street house they continued to cook their meals in South College with everyone else. The children had spent their pre-school years in the friendly environs of the Church of the Redeemer pre-school programme where Susan often worked. There was little time to adjust to the environment of Cumbrae before the new term began for Susan and Gordon's daughter Michal-Ann. Like so many of the other children, she found the change hard to overcome. The Scottish school was strict and authoritarian, tightly organized and structured. Once released onto the playground, pent-up energy erupted in fights and aggressive behaviour. The children from the Cathedral, who were friends with one another regardless of sex or age, were taunted and laughed at. Nor was it possible for parents to visit the children's teachers. They could only arrange to talk with the headmaster, so there was no way for the Community adults to be of much more help to the children.

Things were very different; different from Houston, different from Yeldall, different from anywhere any of them had ever lived before. The Community decided to meet together with the children on a regular basis, to support them, to hear their stories, to share the Community's life as a family, to have fun together. The Community began to hold these family meetings every Sunday afternoon in the South College sitting room.

CHAPTER THREE

Celebrating the Power of God

Last week we experienced what it means to be marooned on an island. We had a terrific storm with fifty to seventy mph winds which lasted four days. The ferries stopped running and the phones in all but one building were dead. Four of us were stuck on the mainland. We sustained no damage and all is well now. It was rather exciting.

Newsletter 27th January 1976

February 29th, 1976. It was Sunday and the wind was blowing fiercely. The conversation around the Community was of an upset in the town; someone had been offended by the Community. At the morning service the second verse of one of the songs had the phrase, 'Oh, let it freely burn....' and Bill Farra prayed for the purifying fire of the Holy Spirit to do just that in the Community.

Lunch that day was a common meal, with everyone gathering in the South College sitting room to eat, to say farewell to some guests who were leaving that afternoon, and to greet the Hopstadius family who had just arrived. After lunch, there was a break in activity before the afternoon gathering for sharing and worship with the children. Each household took a turn in leading the afternoon time, planned as a way for them all to get to know one another more as a community family. Sometimes there was worship, sometimes a household laid on entertainment.

During the break, Jodi Page and Pat Allen crossed to North College in the blustering wind to take a quick nap. Bill Farra gave in to the flu and decided finally to go to bed until he felt better. He and Mimi had one of the larger rooms upstairs in the North College, at the northern end of the building by the stairs down to the kitchen. Several young children were due for an afternoon sleep. The two youngest Hopstadius children were asleep downstairs. Carol Kennedy put Jeremy into his cot for a sleep just three rooms down from where Bill was, nearer still to Jodi and Pat. Carol took Will, her four-year-old son with her. If the need arose, the others in North College would hear Jeremy call and she would come back to check on him and get him up. Down on the shore the local people were gathered watching attempts to salvage a fishing boat that had been wrecked by the storm the previous night.

Pat Allen woke and seeing the time went over to the meeting. Pat decided not to wake Jodi, thinking that she probably needed to catch up on her sleep. Jeremy was still sleeping, and North College was quiet.

Jodi woke with a start, saw from the clock that the meeting was nearly over and the guests were about to leave. She threw on some clothes, the first she could grab. Out in the hallway she listened at Jeremy's door, but he was obviously still asleep. She hurried outside to find Phil and the guests near the car. Goodbyes were said and Jodi wandered into the meeting to catch the end.

Bill stirred. Out of his sleep he could hear Jeremy crying but heard no one else. He struggled into wakefulness, and was instantly alert. He could smell smoke, quite strongly. Climbing out of bed, he grabbed his dressing gown and headed for the door. The hallway was a solid wall of smoke, its acrid fumes choked him. Bill's mind raced through the possibilities and panic welled. He must get to Jeremy, whose cries were of real distress now.

Slamming the door against the smoke, Bill leapt for the back stairs down to the kitchen, three at a time. Outside the wind was icy. He rounded the corner into the full force of the near gale-force wind that beat onto the front of the building. He ran in through the front door and up the stairs. Jeremy's bedroom door was right next to these stairs through the newly fitted fire door. Faced by the same wall of smoke, Bill faltered for just a moment before taking a deep breath and plunging on, feeling for the bedroom door handle. The smoke engulfed him; he tried to see, tried to breathe, but was gagged and choked. Crawling on hands and knees, he finally reached the crib, grabbed the baby and headed for the hall and the stairs and out.

Ed Baggett left the meeting, to burst back in only seconds later.

'North College is on fire! Quick, help!'

Instantly everyone was filled with fear for Bill, for baby Jeremy and the Hopstadius children. Jodi and David Gustafson, nearest the door, moved fast. They ran out of the cloister with the rest of the Community close on their heels. Horrified, they saw that the flames were already burning along the eaves and in the windows at the south end. When they reached the front door, there was Bill, white as a sheet, in just his pyjamas and dressing gown, clutching little Jeremy to his chest. They pulled him away from the building and brought the Swedish children to safety. Carol came and took Jeremy with her into the Annexe building with the other tiny children. At least they were out of the building and safe.

Mimi, six months pregnant, came up to Bill. She had never seen Bill look non-plussed, but it was more than that. He was obviously in shock.

'Bill....'

'I only just got him out.... I nearly didn't get him.... I couldn't get through.... the stairs.... the smoke....'

Shaking with flu and half frozen from the wind, Bill stood in the alley and watched the frenzy of activity.

Someone called the fire brigade and the Community quickly formed a bucket line which led from South College up the fire escape steps and into the door at the rear of North College. That was where the fire was burning most fiercely. Those watching saw the water hurled against the flames that seemed only to leap more fiercely. Joe Thorn and Mikel Kennedy who were at the head of the line choked and vomitted from the heavy smoke. Immediately others took their places. Phil returned from taking the guests to the ferry slip and grabbed keys to the cars parked near North College. He eased them through the crowd to park them where they were out of danger.

The fire was obviously serious, but as the fire engine arrived, everyone sighed with relief. There would be a terrible mess to clear up now, but at least these men could deal with it.

The Cumbrae fire engine had few calls to answer, certainly few fires of this magnitude. The hoses were hauled off the tender and laid out down the hill to the nearest mains connection. A couple of Community members helped. Joining them up was a problem because the entire length of hose was laid out backwards. They turned it around and connected it, losing valuable minutes. Then it was discovered that the hose had holes in it and the water pressure was too low, so instead of a gushing torrent attacking the flames, there was barely a trickle. One of the firemen phoned for the Ardrossan fire-engine to come from the mainland to help fight the fire.

Down on the shore there was much to see. The wreck might be righted before nightfall. A fire engine had passed and there was smoke on the hill. Half an hour later the Ardrossan fire engine raced by and turned up the hill. The crowd changed; something major was going on at the Cathedral. People hurried up the hill to watch the activity or lend a hand if they could.

The flames were now eating through the roof slates. The wind which was picking up hurried them along the attic. Suddenly everyone, instead of thinking the fire would soon be over, realized that the building was going to burn completely.

Some were in tears, distressed and fraught. All who could began to lift furniture and belongings out of the ground floor which included the music office with all its files, chairs and tables, and equipment. Community and local people together grabbed and hauled everything they could lay hands on.

There were many treasured possessions upstairs in the bedrooms. Mikel's guitar was upstairs. Jodi, seeing the fire in the roof exclaimed, 'I've got all my poetry up there, and songs too. I have to get them, they can't be replaced!' Mikel and Jodi both ran for the stairs. She had pictured how to grab her folders and Pat's notebooks and would be outside in seconds. A fireman stood on the stairs; he would let them go no further. It was too late.

The small children who had been herded into the Annexe to keep them safely out of the way were being cared for by Cathleen, Virginia and Carol. They grew more anxious. Will saw his dad, Mikel, sick and choking but couldn't see what was happening. He and the other children were growing hysterical. Virginia took action.

'These children cannot understand. I think it's worse for them to hear all the noise and not know what's happening. I think we should walk them round the Cathedral to where they can see but be at a safe distance.' They donned their coats and Virginia picked up Will. It was slow going right round the Cathedral trailing the tiny ones, but the noise of the fire was covered by the wind. They rounded the corner and Will, shocked, grabbed more tightly round Virginia's neck. He was silent only a moment.

'What about my toys? They're all in there.' Tears showed.

'Don't worry, honey', Virginia reassured him. 'I'm sure we will get you some more somehow.'

Will was quiet; he knew toys cost money. 'Oh well, Aunt Virginia, I suppose we can always make paper aeroplanes.'

The fireman who was monitoring the situation called to those getting the furniture out. 'Everyone out! It is going to go.'

Joe Thorn and other Fisherfolk dropped what they were carrying and ran clear. The roof, flaming along its full length, caved in with a crash and a flurry of sparks and gushing smoke.

Mimi, standing in the shelter of the Lady Chapel, saw the faces of the watching crowd. Some were crying hysterically, some looked angry and despairing. She felt the strengthening wind, like bellows forcing the fire along the roof. The flames filled window after window along the length of the first floor and she saw the shock as person after person lost all that they owned in the world. Her room was last, farthest to the north. The fire reached it. If God had wanted, he could have stopped it; the wind could have blown the other way, or he could calm the wind altogether. The whole drama seemed a mighty act of God and Mimi was not going to argue with God.

Jodi stood sobbing; it was horrible, like watching someone die, and being powerless to do anything about it.

The Booth family lived in Largs, so the ten Fisherfolk hurried into cars to catch the last ferry across. At least they would have somewhere to sleep that night. Though the fire was still blazing and they didn't want to go, they went.

The fire began to die down as night was falling. The firemen continued to spray the smoking ruin, drowning its last attempts to burn. The first floor and the roof were totally ruined. The ground floor was waterlogged. They watched till the end, Community people and Millport people together, shocked and mesmerized. People trailed into the sitting room in South College; the earlier meeting seemed an age ago. They looked at one another's blackened, tear-streaked faces. There were twenty-six homeless people, ten of whom had just caught the last ferry to the mainland. Bill Farra still wore his pyjamas and the old black cassock that served as a dressing gown. It was all he owned now. He saw Mimi in a blue maternity dress; it was a long dress and all right for Sundays. Everything they owned was gone: their clothes, their wedding presents, their photos. There was almost nothing he could do to help; he was still shivering with the flu.

Carter Withey, just fifteen years old, touched Bill's arm.

'Bill, I want to give you these. You'll need more than pyjamas and I think these will fit.'

Carter had just saved up enough pocket money to buy new denim jeans which he had fetched from his room to give to Bill. Others came forward to share what they had.

The local townsfolk found themselves offering more help to these strangers in their midst whose needs were now so pressing and could not be met by the Community itself. The family who ran the pottery, the Swans, took in the Kennedy family, Mikel, Carol, Will and Jeremy, and shared their home with them till alternative accommodation could be found.

On March 1st a gale was really blowing and the Fisherfolk on the mainland watched anxiously for signs that the ferry might run. Eventually there was just one in the evening.

The local Council had a building called the Garrison, midway along the front, that was used for offices. At the back were rooms used for summer holiday accommodation. These rooms were never heated and there were no cooking facilities. The Fisherfolk and others moved in. The cold and damp crept into everyone's bones. The only warm place was in the bath with the hot tap running.

Mimi hated those last weeks of her pregnancy, getting up in the bitter cold and trudging the quarter of a mile up to the Cathedral buildings for breakfast. Life seemed to be too much effort.

One large room at the Garrison contained three double beds. Six women moved in. Lots of people had donated hot water bottles so each bed had four or five in an effort to drive away the dampness and fight the cold. Jodi, sharing a bed with Margi Hackett woke at one a.m. She felt dampness. Her hand felt a leaking and almost flat hot water bottle. So there was the cause! The dampness was still warm; she was tempted not to move, but the water was bound to cool later in the night. She nudged Margi and woke the others.

'We have to come in and join you. Sorry about it, but there's nothing else we can do.'

Jodi caught laryngitis and moved to South College to sleep on someone's bedroom floor where it was a little warmer. She went to the surgery a day or two later. Several local people were already in the waiting room, so Jodi took one of the remaining chairs and began to flip through a magazine. No one recognized her, except Elizabeth Swan from the pottery who smiled at Jodi when she entered. The other occupants were discussing the recent events with vigour. 'We've had those buildings for a hundred and twenty-five years and it took a bunch of damn Yankees just a year to burn them down.' Jodi stayed still and quiet, embarrassed for them and for herself.

Many members of the Community helped to pick through the debris to see what could be salvaged. The upper floor had burned completely and the ground floor was waterlogged. Mimi looked over the blackened mess that was her and Bill's bedroom. The antique furniture was charred and ruined, but a modern, ill-made desk set in an alcove was all right. Inside the desk she found the tin that held the household's cash. It held the thirty pound notes undamaged. Judith was helping Mimi sift through the ashes, and found Mimi's wedding ring unharmed beneath four inches of rubble. The bed had collapsed, more water-logged than burned. Some things had been stored beneath it. There Mimi found her wedding photos, a little wet, but otherwise safe.

Those who lived in the North College household lost nearly everything. Mostly Americans, they had brought with them mementoes of family and friends, enough to fit in a box under their beds. Now these were gone. But as word was passed around, people all over the country, all over the world began to send gifts, clothes, blankets and household equipment. Some were close friends: St Michael's at York, the Community at Yeldall Manor, Post Green in Dorset. Others were strangers. One person sent a tiny box, containing six wrist watches. Post Green sent a truck laden with clothes. Someone sent Bibles. A lady in America sent a copy of a book Jodi had been reading while staying at her house a year previously; she was sure Jodi had lost it. People in the States sent photos to replace lost ones.

The Community at Yeldall packed an enormous box to

send by Red Star on British Rail, so it would get immediate delivery within a day. It took half a dozen people to squeeze it into a minibus. Edward Prebble drove to the station. 'We'll take it', said the Red Star agent, 'if one person can put it on the scales.' The scales were only six inches off the ground, but a long way from the van. Edward was not going to take the box home again. He would do it somehow. He levered the box, which was five feet by five feet, from the van and with immense effort managed to roll it along the platform and onto the scales. The agents looked on, startled, but Edward managed it. Bob Morris picked up the box at the station in Glasgow and somehow got it into the Cumbrae minibus and so onto the island.

There were investigations, but the cause of the fire was never fully determined. It may have been an electrical fault; the wiring was old and in need of replacement. Or it could have been a coal falling from an open fire. The insurance company checked over the building and the work crew began to clear it. The Fisherfolk training programme, Phil's reason for being at the Community, had ended with the fire, so he and others moved in with shovels and spades. They took everything to the rubbish tip, saving only what would burn in the fires that heated other households. The wet and stormy Cumbrae weather would soon rot the damaged and unprotected building so plastic sheeting was spread throughout the upper floor to catch the rain. The water that collected each day was siphoned out and on the ground floor all the fires were kept burning to dry out what was left. Builders did not arrive till August.

On the day of the fire the Fisherfolk had been midway through the rehearsal schedule for a new recording which was to be made at the end of March. They continued rehearsing, praying that the wind would stay away while they worked.

The title of the recording was 'Celebrate the whole of it'. The title song itself was a challenge 'For the joy and for the sorrow, yesterday, today, tomorrow, we celebrate'. The fire was to them part of their life with God, of going on faithfully, doing his will, and celebrating not only all the good things he had given them, but celebrating even the fire.

Ruth had saved ashes from Pat and Jodi's room and the Community used them for the Ash Wednesday service to mark a cross on each person's forehead.

CHAPTER FOUR

A Calling to Life and Ministry

We have received so many gifts of clothing, money and other articles lost in the fire.... I have been very moved by many of the letters. One man wrote, 'We do not agree with what you preach and the way you live, but out of the love of Christ for our brothers in need we send this gift.' We have been overwhelmed by the love of so many brothers that we don't even know. The Lord is good!

Newsletter 26th April 1976

The spring came and North College was still only a damaged shell. Accommodation was cramped and awkward for members of the Community of Celebration. In July, there was to be the double wedding of Margi Hackett and Bill Pulkingham, Martha Keys and Conway Barker who were all members of the Fisherfolk team. It was also the year of the Musical.

After the recording of 'Celebrate the whole of it' the Fisherfolk packed their bags again and moved south to Yeldall Manor where part of the Community still remained and where there was room to rehearse and room to live. After a spell in Sweden, working at a conference centre, the team returned to Cumbrae. Caravans had been acquired and permission had been received to locate these temporarily in the field behind the Annexe. Work began on the musical which was to be performed at the Edinburgh Festival Fringe.

Each year at the Edinburgh Festival there is an addition to the main events, a fringe festival. Many artists and performers, both professional and amateur, many innovative or radical, were included in the Fringe.

Phil had been back to Chorleywood, planning to stay there permanently; he found the church very different from the year before, and after a few weeks returned to Cumbrae. He arrived in time to work on the musical. Mikel, Martha and Pat Beall already had a plot in mind. Now they drew together the Fisherfolk team. There was still a shortage of space, so the Swans came to the rescue again and loaned the Community their pottery, an old church building, to use for the rehearsals. The cast and crew included the Fisherfolk, some of the trainees like Phil, and some long-term guests from Sweden. From the basic plot, the cast themselves improvised and developed the actual script. Mikel wrote several new songs and many older numbers were included.

Little Graham Farra was born in May 1976, just three months after the fire. Having had a successful career in music including her work with Betty on *Sound of Living Waters* and *Fresh Sounds,* Mimi was happy to spend time at home raising a family. The baby was born with his feet turned in, a problem that could be corrected with a simple operation when he was a little older. However, his vomitting was more distressing. After every feed he vomitted as soon as he was moved. For months, until he was ten months old in fact, Mimi had to stick to old clothes and very few other people really wanted to pick him up! Yet he was a sweet and friendly baby.

Preparations were under way for the double wedding. Bill and Conway's families, members of the Community, were already there, and Margi's and Martha's parents planned to come over from the States for the occasion. Friends were expected from all over Britain. Since accommodation was still so limited, some of the guests were prepared to camp on the lawns. The catering, one of the biggest jobs of all, was being planned well in advance.

Betty had been doing her own special preparation. A few months before the wedding she asked Bill if there were some special Bible verses around which she could compose a wedding anthem. He came back to her with verses from Isaiah and she added a few more. These became the anthem, 'For ye shall go out with joy.' For Betty the words and music were an expression of God's word to his people who, in obedience, go out to do his bidding and then experience deserts being turned to places that bloom.

Just days before the wedding the team broke off their rehearsal schedule for the musical, by now named, 'Ah, there's the celebration.' They worked night and day to complete all the details: bouquets were arranged, vases filled, food baked and tables prepared, and the Cathedral cleaned and polished for the service. So many people were coming for the wedding on the fourth of July that the Cathedral would be overflowing. All the chairs were removed. There was standing room only to fit everyone in.

The morning of the wedding dawned clear and calm. The weather on Cumbrae was at best unpredictable. Often it was cold and wet even in the height of summer. God seemed to be smiling on them that day. It remained sunny and warm throughout the day.

The service was reminiscent of festivals in the Old Testament, rich and exhilarating, full of music and joy. Graham preached and the two couples performed their own wedding dance. Bishop Wimbush, now near retirement, was in attendance. Betty, among the musicians, looked over at him and saw him in tears, moved by the very beautiful service. Children were everywhere involved with everyone else, dressed in their best. A couple of younger boys disappeared minutes after the church service to reappear in their usual play clothes for rolling around on the grass!

Food was served from South College and people gathered all over the south lawns and danced together. Some of their local friends, the Swans and others, joined in Scottish folk dancing and American square-dancing.

With four members of the cast away on their honeymoons, rehearsals were interrupted. While they were gone, the rest of the team made props and painted them. Being extremely busy helped minimize the hardness of the living situation which was difficult until North College was fully restored. As a listed historic building, it had to be rebuilt exactly to its previous state, and that would take some time.

When the honeymooners returned the musical was completed. An advance group went over to Edinburgh to check over the practical arrangements. Old St Paul's Church had regularly been involved in the Edinburgh Festival Fringe and hosted events in their building. 'Ah, there's the celebration' was performed there daily. The Fisherfolk team had often dreamed of putting their talents into a musical so this was the culmination of several years of creative thinking. Most of the team were relatively inexperienced at working with drama of this kind, normally focusing their skills on the needs of worship.

The story was strong, full of colourful characters. Jesus sat on a high stool overlooking the playing area, singing to encourage and teach his people as the story unfolded. The family of clowns in the story were under pressure from a nasty but quite plausible devil to change and be just as selfish and greedy as the rest of the world. They wished simply to receive new members into the Family. There were lots of unpleasant ploys and tricks from 'Devv', but of course he didn't win in the end. The whole story was a parable of the Community's calling and lifestyle. The musical was so successful and well received that equipment was set up and a live recording was made at an evening performance. The cast left for the United States as soon as the Festival was over so that they could present the musical at the triennial National Convention of the Episcopal Church.

Some of the people who had been technical help in Edinburgh came back to Cumbrae rather than going to the States. Work was continuing on the renovation of the buildings. The refectory, part of the South College, was being stripped of old stain. Phil was at the top of a ladder scraping the ceiling when the ladder broke; he found himself on the floor upside down, with the ladder on top of him. Leslie Roberts, coming in the door from the office, was absolutely horrified, convinced he had broken his neck. As he fell, Phil swore at the top of his voice, and once on the floor was convinced he had broken his leg. The doctor came to discover Phil had actually broken his right arm. The guest who had unfortunately heard the swear words left almost immediately; Phil never saw him again, and was never quite sure if the man left the Community because of the swearing, or because he was scheduled to leave anyway. Phil recovered quickly and, in answer to his prayers, was back working within a week.

Perhaps it was because Mimi and Bill were first-time parents and were aware of Graham's already diagnosed condition that they noticed nothing amiss. At three months, however, Mimi found herself worried. There were odd things. Graham responded excitedly to toys in his pram and hit out at them with his hands, but though he smiled when she picked him up or when she spoke to him,

Mimi began to realize he didn't follow her with his eyes. There was no eye contact. Mimi moved a lamp across Graham's line of vision and there was no response. She went into hers and Bill's bedroom.

'Bill, I think Graham is blind.' She managed to say it calmly.

Bill's response was hard for her to take. 'If he is, I'm sure it is so the Lord can be glorified.'

Inside, Mimi's heart was thumping. 'Oh yuk!' she thought to herself. 'How can it be that simple?'

Through the next few weeks when the doctors examined and diagnosed Graham, Virginia was encouraging. She and Mimi talked and worked at what it meant for the Community to have a blind child among them.

The doctors diagnosed Graham as sightless, that is, there was no specific medical reason for the blindness. He simply could not see. Mimi began to read books on blind children, struggling at the same time with her own emotional response to the situation. She began to accept the circumstance enough to talk to more doctors. One doctor in Edinburgh was researching a sonar apparatus that could be strapped to the forehead, but it was too cumbersome for a small baby.

Mimi grieved, numbed by it all. Everyone prayed. Jodi and the rest of the Fisherfolk Team in the States began to join their prayers as soon as they heard the news.

According to the books on child development, twenty weeks was a critical time. Until then, a blind child develops much as any other, but after that time, general development is so closely related to visual awareness that blind children begin to lose ground. Graham reached twenty weeks.

Bill crept carefully into Graham's room to see if he was awake. Graham turned his head and looked straight at his dad. Bill stopped in his tracks and, scarcely believing what was happening, went out of the room. He was sure that he had made no sound. He waited a while and then cautiously stepped into the room again. Graham turned, looked straight at Bill and smiled.

Graham could see!

The doctors said it was a spontaneous beginning of sight. They did not know why, but sometimes it happens. It was apparently a miracle that Graham could now see. But as Mimi reflected on God's gift to Graham, she realized that in each of us, sight is a miracle, one we take for granted, but no less a miracle.

Graham grew up with sensitive hearing, a compensation for his time of sightlessness. There were still some problems that necessitated surgery later and his binocular vision is still not quite right.

When he was two Graham went to hospital for an operation on his feet. A cut was made that allowed the muscles to stretch and his feet to straighten. He came home with both legs in plaster and David Gustafson built him a little truck, very low to the ground, so Graham could push himself along with his hands. He found it great fun.

In the States, the Fisherfolk travelled extensively, training teams of worship leaders and visiting several churches. One stop was with the Community of Celebration in Woodland Park, Colorado to have a break and spend time with friends and family as well as work with the Community's Fisherfolk team to develop its ministry. It was time for a well-deserved rest. The year had been dramatic and at times traumatic for the Fisherfolk. Their home and all their belongings were lost in the fire. The musical was an intense creative adventure, but wearying. The wedding had been a rich celebration. Little Graham Farra, one of the first Fisherfolk children, had been born both crippled and blind. Everyone was extremely tired.

It required enormous effort to pack yet again and fly back to Britain.

Once home, the team began to say they had travelled too long without any real home. A change was needed in the schedules and in the pattern of their life. They were able to share their weariness with the whole Community family. After so much travelling it was hard to feel at home in Cumbrae, even though that was where they were housed; the team had never had the chance to settle in.

It was a relief for those in the travelling ministry, who were used to living in the limelight, to step off the ferry into a town where they were nobody in particular. They wanted to be at home and ordinary. It was hard, however, for them to come home and find the Community at odds with and sometimes rejected by a vociferous minority among the islanders.

The Community's relationship with the town was a constant concern. It was hard for the small town community to receive newcomers. These new people, in addition to being culturally different, with their American origins, had their own community around which their life revolved. It was doubly difficult for the two communities to either understand one another or become enmeshed in a constructive way. Lack of communication brought tensions for individuals and caused considerable hurt. Neither the local people nor members of the Community could really understand each other. They could only make assumptions about motives, with more or less charity.

Behind the Garrison on the sea front there was a little coffee shop. The previous occupants had been Youth with a Mission. The Community managed to obtain the lease and for the summer wanted to run the shop to make contact with both local people and tourists. Some local residents, however, found the work offensive and considered it a violation of the agreed use of the building. The local paper even carried an article with the headline 'Evict the American Evangelists'. Though some local people wrote letters to the local paper in support of the Community's activities, the lease was withdrawn.

The ways in which the Community was seen by the townsfolk were interpreted in the language they knew. The Community members hugged one another in public, which was not at all usual in Millport, and local people were shocked to learn that two men had hugged each other on the ferry slip. This new group at the Cathedral seemed just as strange as some of the earlier residents.

When local families had taken Community members into their homes after the fire, friendships had been made between individuals. But it was more difficult for local people to get to know the whole Community as a family or to understand how and why it operated the way it did. To some extent, they found the Community's organization and the businesses rather unfriendly. In struggling to get the threads of its life together, it was necessary for the Community to have a well-defined administration and management structure. Though local people found individuals very friendly, the Fisherfolk who had the greatest involvement with the public were regularly absent from the island. The local people just could not understand it, all they saw was the movement. Trying to unravel these points of tension caused considerable stress.

The Community decided it was time to review the situation. What was happening, they asked themselves? Why had God brought them here? What was God saying to them? They had moved from Yeldall Manor, lost their possessions in the fire, and some island people were openly hostile about their presence.

A week was set aside for fasting, prayer and discussion. Three aspects of life were under specific consideration: what was the Community's particular calling in ministry;

what was the strategy for fulfilling this ministry; and what were the Community's needs at home? They met for six hours during the day and another two hours in the evenings when the older children joined them.

The discussion went on through the week. All the concerns, worries and frustrations were shared: the travelling ministry, the isolation they felt, the homelessness some experienced, and their relationship to Millport. Would God speak to them and bring some change?

The week drew to a close and finished with a celebration of the Eucharist. As the service proceeded, Jodi realized that God was giving her a picture to share with the group.

The vision revealed a woodland glen, an open space between the trees. The sun shone between the branches and leaves onto a beautiful and exotic flower. The petals were poppy red; at the heart was a gold star-shaped stamen. The plant was delicate and seemed fragile, vulnerable.

A movement began, the flower closed up and withdrew into a cluster of three trees. Spiders' webs came across the vision, hiding the plant from view. Clouds covered the sun and rain fell, pouring heavily, washing baby birds out of their nests in the trees to the right. The sun reappeared, drying up the puddles from the rain, but the nestlings were left chirping and hungry. Jodi was aware then of a rumbling beneath the ground where the roots of the flower were pushing through the soil. With a sense of explosive, volcanic energy flowing through the roots of the plant and up through the stem, a bud burst from the cobwebs into the glen. The petals opened. The gold stamen had been crushed into grain which poured out into the mouths of the baby birds. The flower was no longer beautiful and fragile but had the sturdier, tougher look of a succulent. The grain coming from it was flowing like water from a garden hose.

The elders had a long meeting to discuss the meaning of the vision in light of the previous week's conversation. They called the Community back together. For the last few years, the Community and the Fisherfolk had been in the limelight. Churches and organizations for renewal had received many blessings through the ministry. The music books *Sound of Living Waters* and *Fresh Sounds* were widely known. Fisherfolk records were best-sellers among Christian records. After being so popular, being centre stage, God was now saying, 'It's time to get the stars out of your eyes. It is time to settle down into ordinary life.'

Everyone had been moving around for years. Some had arrived as students and had never had an ordinary job or a regular schedule. Some had now married and children were on the way. There were now four babies in the Community under a year old. All the adults seemed stressed by the pace of life and wanted to 'put roots down'.

The Community questioned the ministry to people around the world. They wished to preach a quality of friendship and family to the Christians they met, but found it hard to know what they really had to say when their financial base was so different. The Community lived on donations and some income from the music business. There were those outside the Community who could not see how the Celebration lifestyle had validity for those ordinary church people who had ordinary jobs.

The Community decided that they would put down roots in Millport and restrict their travelling ministry as much as possible. It was a considerable change to make, from being international troubadours. The music business producing records and books was promising. More effort could go into that. The financial base of the Community, primarily its source of income, was also going to change.

They would find a way to make their own income, to become eventually self-supporting. Some churches in the States had been committing large sums of money as donations to the Community. The Community decided it was time to ask these churches to stop supporting them in this way. Not surprisingly, they found those who had given so generously were hearing the same word from God. Some donations would continue to come in, as would covenants, but hopefully as a more balanced aspect of financial stability.

And what about the relationship to Millport and having more contact with the local people? Someone pointed out that the bakery in the town was up for sale.

CHAPTER FIVE

Bake Bread with the Fisherfolk

Business as usual (just about). On 27th August the bakery will provide junk food for a party of 100 children. Pat Allen and Ed Baggett work at Kames Bay Branch. Takings have been increasing daily. A relaxed atmosphere in the bakehouse was noted: nothing is 'burned'—it is all 'well-fired'.

Community Forum, 10th August 1977

The owner of Speirs Bakery was the last of a family that had owned and operated the bakery for a hundred years. He had no children to follow him and so wanted to sell up and retire. There seemed to be few interested buyers. Millport had suffered in recent years as people became more affluent and adventurous about holidays so travelled further away from Scotland. At one time it had been cheaper living on the tiny island off the coast. Now with contemporary employment patterns and rising consumer standards, it had become more expensive to live on Cumbrae. A greater proportion of commodities were brought over on the ferry to sell in the shops so should have been a few pence more expensive. Yet customers expected lower prices on the island, so the shops sustained lower profits. Retail businesses were not easy to sell. Some representatives of the Community of Celebration approached the baker.

As with all small towns, news—especially bad news—travels fast. Local people had noticed that the Community had bought property. The house in George Street had been the beginning. Other houses had been purchased. Now with a possible take-over in the bakery, it was obvious they intended to control the whole island in the future. Anxieties and rumours spoke of drastic possibilities.

The agreement between Speirs Bakery and the Community was finalized and a take-over date was set. As a preparatory stage, four of the Fisherfolk, Bill and Margi Pulkingham, Conway Barker and Richard Gullen, began to work for the baker to learn the routines. None of them had any previous experience. They were learning from scratch and began to do day-release courses in Glasgow to qualify as bakers.

Bill and Margi Pulkingham were to manage the business. There were some local people on the staff of the shop, most of whom had decided to leave before the change-over. One seasonal employee stayed through to the end of the summer. A few staff stayed on though they faced criticism from other townsfolk. Jack Penders, master baker, stayed right through and kept things going while nearly everyone else was learning the trade.

Meanwhile, a large ministry team had gone to live in Detroit in the States for ten weeks to share the lifestyle of the Community with a newly formed group, Precious Blood Community. With days to go to the bakery change-over it was obvious more staff would be needed. Phil, who had returned from the ministry in Detroit and was now rewiring and doing other maintenance to the buildings, was asked if he would join the bakery staff. He lived in South College with those already working in the bakery and he saw how tired they were after long, hard shifts. He was not at all sure he wanted to join them, at least not permanently, but agreed to try it.

Jack made a suggestion that the new bakers were each paired with only one of the skilled employees, as a means of learning specific skills. Some, like Phil, who were quite adept with their hands, were soon able to match the speed of the more experienced staff.

The take-over came in August and caught the tail end of the summer season when there were still quite a few tourists. The first few days were chaotic. Inside the bakery there was considerable confusion; lots of mistakes were made; the stocks were running low; too much of particular lines had been baked. The Community households did not mind the latter as they were now the recipients of any leftovers!

Some industrial action, almost unheard of on this peaceful island, accompanied the take-over of the bakery. It was rumoured that a couple of local people stood outside the main shop on the Community's first day of ownership and urged others not to go in to buy their bread. Most knew how important the bakery was to the economy of the island, however, and business went on as usual. Within two years, the bakery was able to provide a substantial proportion of the Community's finances.

Summer drew to an end and the demand for bread and cakes fell drastically. The staff, most of whom had been travelling Fisherfolk, were then needed as much as possible to participate in the recording choir. In the winter, shifts could be shorter, work could start later and all the bread could be baked more quickly. During this first winter of baking, the staff joined the rest of the choir, with Betty and Mimi, to make the recording of 'God make us your family'.

The winter recording time became a regular part of the Community's seasonal schedule. Though the off-season was the best time to catch the greatest number of available Community members, it was not necessarily ideal for recording in the Cathedral. Winter is the season of storms and dramatic weather, and everyone prayed that the wind would be still during actual recording sessions. It was remarkable how many times the weather conditions were just right.

Usually the taping for an entire album was completed in two or three days. The choir would be well rehearsed, having spent weeks or months with Mimi and Betty going over all the details of arrangement, instrumentation, and the actual schedule. Ray Prickett, the sound engineer for all the Fisherfolk recordings, travelled up from the London area bringing with him the necessary mobile, multi-track recording equipment. The Cathedral was transformed into a recording studio, with huge screens placed along the walls to deaden the reverberation, and instruments and lead wires and microphones strung from one end of the choir to the other. There were always lots of hot water bottles and blankets. Even if the wind was calm, the Cathedral was still bitterly cold because the cranky and noisy heating system could not be turned on during the actual recording.

Not all of these winter recording sessions occurred on the island. One record of anthems entitled 'Lo, He Comes!' was to be made in Paisley Abbey. On the morning the choir was due to leave the island to begin recording, a fierce gale was blowing and had been for several days. No ferries were running. Undaunted, one of the Community phoned a local fisherman and hired him and his boat to transport the choir across the rough sea to Largs. They were not sure what type of boat they would get, but imagined a cabin with some protection from the rain. The choir gathered at the north end of the island to meet a very small fishing boat, completely open with no cabin. The arrival at Largs was accomplished, though everyone was a little wet.

In the winter when the bakery lost money rather than made it, those still working could become quite disheartened with the anti-social hours that seemed to achieve nothing for the Community financially. The staff had to encourage one another with the perspective of the year's total earnings. As Community members began to have more predictable work schedules, so the music business settled more firmly too. The erratic pattern produced by a high level of travelling ministry began to disappear and along with it part of the stress. The pattern and identity of the Community's life was more compatible with the number of families with small children. Stability and routine were necessary elements. The households became smaller and the groupings more permanent, more readily organized and with easier communication. The tension between household life and business began to settle.

Towards the spring, in March, the bakery began to look forward to the beginning of the new summer season. Then, just before Easter and the hot-cross-bun busy time, the boiler of one of the ovens stopped working. An electrician came and diagnosed the need for a replacement pump. It was delivered and fitted, but to the frustration of the staff, it was not heating fast enough. On Easter Monday brown bread was still being taken from the oven at four p.m.! Most of these early tourists were only weekend visitors and would leave that evening. There was no one to buy the bread! It wasn't till the main peak sales of summer were almost on them that the electrician managed to get the right pump and fit it.

The frustration caused by the late batches of bread provoked innovation. The Community staff now knew enough of the bakery skills to discover new ways to work. Conway and Phil began a night shift; they began work at eleven p.m. First they tackled all the bread orders, then moved on to the bread rolls. They worked right through the night and by seven in the morning had the breadstuffs on the shelves in the shop which opened at 7:30 a.m. They went off to bed at nine a.m. then got up in time to have a meal with their household and spend the evening with the family. The new night shift was so successful they continued to run it right through the summer even though the pump was mended.

The business included two shops. The main shop was the front of the bakehouse and opened onto the sea front not far from the pier. On Kames Bay was a smaller branch shop that served the local estate. The shops were open from 7:30 a.m. to 5 p.m. In winter the shops closed on Monday and Wednesday afternoons.

The bakery, through the presence of Bob Morris who became manager of the main shop and Louise Jolly who ran the branch shop, brought a level of friendship with the local people that could not have been predicted. In a town like Millport, everyone goes into the bakery at some time to buy bread It is the best kind of shop to be in for meeting people. Both Bob and Louise were recognized by the townsfolk as Christians from the Cathedral. Bob found that people got to know him just as a person first, and only later discovered he was a priest. It was a helpful way for the congregation and neighbours to realize there is no need to put a priest on a pedestal, that he is human like everyone else. The townsfolk also got to know more of the Community's children. Clare, Bob's daughter, enjoyed going down to the shop to meet the local people who came in to buy bread and would help her dad make up orders that would later be delivered by the van.

Being priest to the Cathedral was not readily compatible with running a shop. On some days, like Ash Wednesday or Good Friday, extra church services were necessary even though the shop was open. Easter weekend is unusually hard work for a priest. Yet it was also one of the busiest weekends for the bakery. Bob stood at the counter serving thousands of hot-cross-buns till his legs were aching. Then at the last minute he would throw off his apron, rush up to the Cathedral, throw on his vestments and lead the service. The benediction barely spoken, he would reverse the whole procedure and in moments be serving up hot-cross-buns again. There was little time to prepare sermons. Bob improvised a lot, using stories from the bakery shop as sermon illustrations which brought an earthy, ordinary perspective into the Community's worship life.

Some of Bob's innovations in the main shop were very trying for the local people. When he began working in the shop he found there were two tills, one for local people, and one for tourists, with signs telling people to which they should go. There was always a long queue for the tourist till. Bob abolished the system, so only wholesale customers could jump the queue to get their goods quickly. For a while the atmosphere was difficult.

The relationships between the Community and the town were slowly improving, however. Community members began to join local organizations and bakery customers visited the Cathedral and households. Phil made friends with his own age-group on the island and began to help with the Youth Club. When business was slow, the customers often stood and chatted with those behind the counter.

Margaret Duthie was one such customer.

Margaret (or Granny as she is known by many) had lived on the island most of her life and she continued to live in a close by the sea front not far from the shops. She was nearly seventy. It was not far to the bakery branch shop and Granny was a regular customer. Pat Allen and Ed Baggett soon recognized her from among the Kames

Bay shoppers. On a slow day in the shop, Granny found herself talking of her own concerns for her family and friends.

'Would you like us to pray for you?' asked Pat.

Some weeks later Granny went to the mid-week Eucharist. There was lots of singing and teaching, followed by the Eucharist. All the households made contributions to the common meal that followed. This was a new kind of worship for Granny, worship where she was a part of the service with time to voice her own prayers, to pray for her grandson who had been in a car accident. Granny became a regular attender at the Cathedral on Sundays as well as mid-week, and in her seventieth year was confirmed alongside several Community members and young people from Millport. Many of those like Granny who came to the bakery for bread found new life for themselves at the Cathedral of the Isles.

Bill and Margi succeeded in keeping both management in the bakery and worship life together. They maintained their commitments to choir and other aspects of worship leadership and so brought the concerns of the bakery, its staff and its customers, to the heart of the Community. The interests and crises of working life at the bakery were made a part of the life of the rest of the Community and its relationship with God.

For some Community members the change to local life and the bakery had been traumatic. Many had come from the United States straight into quite large Community households. For a while North and South College each had more than twenty people working out life as one family. This involved lots of discussion and planning together and often there was misunderstanding or bad communication. This brought stresses of a particular kind on their family life. Readjustment was necessary. At the same time the life the members thought they had chosen, a travelling worship ministry with the Fisherfolk, had changed.

Coming to the United Kingdom in the early days of the Community of Celebration was like becoming a missionary. People were coming to join a missionary outpost in a foreign country; to tell the good news to those who had not heard it. The proclamation was in a style of life that was visible and tangible. Jodi's vision had foretold the change, becoming rooted deeply and firmly in the land, becoming not missionaries living at a mission station, but making home where they were. Since they now lived in Scotland, this meant embracing the Scottish way of life. Had they known this, there might have been questions about moving to Britain. God was giving the Community a new direction and some members moved back across the ocean to rejoin their churches and families.

At the bakery the staff grew accustomed to the working pattern. The summer, though extremely busy, brought a great sense of satisfaction. Everyone knew that their work was a major contribution to the Community's livelihood and that made the hard work seem worthwhile. It was not always easy. The employees who had been baking for many, many years found it hard to adopt new methods. The new and the old learned to work together with tolerance of one another.

The hoped-for stabilizing of life was beginning to be effective. Life had pattern and order. The music business was able to stabilize its working hours and able more readily to work to defined schedules and deadlines. The work on copyrights of music, till now still in the south, was moved to Cumbrae. The department took on all the administration of royalties and copyrights for *Sound of Living Waters*, *Fresh Sounds* and the new book *Cry Hosanna.* Many letters also came as churches asked permission to use Celebration songs in their church books, or publishers asked for permission to use music in other collections of songs of renewal.

The realization of the first part of Jodi's vision was almost complete. The routine of having people at work early in the morning, coming home very tired after a hard day, a schedule of worship and play and seasons, was quite different from the old scheme of rehearsals, travelling, ministry, meeting and talking with new people all the time. God had made their work life, school life and worship life ordered and compatible in a way that it had never been before.

CHAPTER SIX

Getting onto the Land

> *. . . . overgrown areas have been cleared, the vegetable garden has been cleared, ploughed and made ready for spring planting, the greenhouse has been repaired and is in use, trees have been pruned and flower beds planted.*
>
> Newsletter Autumn 1976

Preparing food for thirty-five, and later seventy-five or more people, required more than a little organization. An order had to be set. Meals for all households, except the George Street house who had begun to use their own kitchen, were served in the crypt adjacent to the kitchen. It had been transformed into a dining room, dark but cosy. Menu planning required considerable effort and organization in order to maintain a balanced and economical diet for so many people.

During this period of the common kitchen in South College there had always been a couple of people who did the shopping. This involved major expeditions to Glasgow. David Porter had moved from Post Green Community and began to shop. He lived in North College and became cook for the large household there. David Stayner, newly arrived from the States, worked with Dave, and found out just how different Britain was.

Twice a week the two of them got up in time to climb into the old minibus, and by 7:15 would be driving to the ferry slip to catch the first boat of the morning. The minibus had seen better days; it had once been the Fisherfolk travelling vehicle but now the seats were gone and the paintwork marked by shifting coke and garden equipment. Mechanically too it needed jollying along.

Dave Porter had an unusual shopping system, at least so it seemed to David Stayner. At each of the markets, fish, meat, vegetables, he had a carrier bag with the necessary cards, lists and money ready to do business. David had discovered the meaning of the carrier bags days before when shopping for himself. Any American making their first excursion into the shops is astonished to find their groceries placed by the cashier in a miscellaneous heap before them. Where were all the sturdy brown bags that every American store provides? If you want a bag, you have to buy a carrier bag of flimsy polythene.

Once at the market, Dave wandered around nonchalantly peering into the boxes and stalls. He assessed what he wanted and then rather indirectly began to bargain with the manager for a better deal than was being offered.

After several visits, David became frustrated with the indirect approach, primarily because he could hardly tell what Dave was trying to buy. He soon tried his own very direct approach, asking for exactly what he wanted. This time, Dave was angry. To him, the approach was brash and unhelpful. It took a while, not without heated exchanges, for them to realize that the men at the market were perfectly happy with either approach.

The minibus arrived back in the afternoon, and was unloaded into South College. The next few hours were spent dividing up the goods, slicing meat, weighing vegetables and delivering it all to the various households, by then located in various parts of the town.

As the Community settled into the island, several houses were purchased, each with smaller households and greater autonomy in their finances and organization. South College was only used for joint Community events, and guests stayed in its corridor of bedrooms. Some ground floor rooms were also used for offices and practice rooms.

Dividing and delivering the shopping seemed unnecessarily time-consuming and many households wanted more variety and choice in their menu. Yet, the bargains were often the result of the bulk quantities being bought. If everyone organized their own buying it would be easier on Dave and David. But how could there be a halfway stage between the central buying system and having each household send someone off the island to do shopping in Glasgow? The Community decided to continue the economical bulk buying, but set up a co-op where households would individually make their purchases from the items purchased by Dave and David.

At the back of the main bakery shop there was an unused store room, an old wooden building. It was made available for them to use. Dave found some shelving up at the Cathedral and set it up so the old storeroom could be run as a food shop to the Community. Only one trip to Glasgow per week was necessary for restocking the shelves and households collected their own perishable goods on the day they were bought.

Convenient and economical as this system turned out to be, it did not suit everyone. The local shopkeepers saw all this happening, saw the Community of about seventy-five people doing all its buying off the island. The Scots are not a people who keep their grumbles to themselves; they tell you if you have offended them and are willing to openly sort out the problems. It was not very English and Dave found the comments the local greengrocer shouted across the street at them really quite disturbing. David was less upset but as the comments increased he thought something must change. Once a young woman from the Community came home in tears after a conversation with one local resident. Dave and David finally brought their concern to the entire Community that they might pray for a solution.

A few days later Bill Farra was walking along the sea front with David on the way to the bakery when Hector called out to them, 'When are you folk going to come down off the hill, and start doing business in our shops, instead of keeping yourselves to yourselves?'

To David's surprise Bill responded, 'If you think we're isolated up on the hill, why don't you come up to see us instead of only expecting us to come down to you?'

There was a stunned silence. Bill crossed the street. 'Would you like to come up to dinner and meet all of us? Come to North College one evening, and bring your wife.'

Though taken aback, Hector accepted.

There were twenty-two people living in North College, several of them children. Hector and his wife arrived, bearing a good size bottle of wine as a gift, and were met at the door by little Graham Farra. Graham loved guests and Hector loved children. They made friends very quickly. Once supper was over they all sat around and sang for one another and Hector recited some poetry.

The friendship changed things. Hector offered to buy vegetables in bulk for them; it was an offer too good to refuse. It was the beginning of shopping for all groceries on the island. Dave and David still did the shopping, but went to Hector's once a week to place the Community order. They would sit for hours chatting with Hector in the back-room behind his shop. The Community and the island were getting closer to one another.

As households began to frequent the local shops, the Community store began to wind down. There was less work to do to keep it running and staff were needed elsewhere. Val Nobbs took over the store and within a few weeks closed it down. Dave moved into the bakery and made scones all summer.

David and a team of people began making sandwich lunches for the whole Community including the summer visitors. During the summer there were lots and lots of guests, from Sweden, America and Australia. Many of the guests helped maintain the Cathedral property, mowing the lawns, trimming hedges, cutting and tidying the undergrowth between the Cathedral and George Street.

The 'grounds crew' into which all the guests were drawn was headed up by Mike Cockayne, an Australian priest. Mike was with the Community for a while to learn and prepare for beginning a community in Australia. With all the workers available the grounds were slowly transformed, neatened and replanted. However, to the north of the property was the barn and adjacent couple of acres of land. Since being left by the previous tenant they had become covered in weeds. So Mike bought a goat—one milking goat.

As the summer drew on towards autumn, so the busy bakery schedule slowed down and Dave looked for a break from its routine. He was offered the opportunity to take over from Mike, who was due to return to Australia. Dave's first task was to learn to milk the goat. He had done mowing before and picked apples and pulled weeds; care of the grounds was straightforward. But milking a goat was quite strange for someone who had grown up in Liverpool.

David's lunch-making duties had ended with the departure of the summer visitors, so he began to work with Dave again. They called it 'The Farm'; a few acres of land, a broken-down barn, and one goat.

David had hated the farm he had grown up on as a child and swore he would never get involved with dairy farming again. And it seemed ridiculous to have one milking goat and seventy-five people! It didn't make good farming sense to him at all. He decided, despite his feelings about farming, that if they got more goats the farm could provide milk for the whole Community. The subject was raised at several meetings. Everyone was asked whether they would be committed to drinking goat's milk if it was produced. Some did not like it, others did not mind. After all, if it was drunk really fresh and very cold, it was all right. But there was a strong taste quite quickly. The Community gave the go-ahead for the plan, though various people, like Leslie Roberts, never did get accustomed to it. Little Graham and Michelle Farra drank it almost all of their lives so they did not really like cow's milk. David and Dave continued making their plans for the farm.

Although having goats was much like the dairy farming David grew up with, he and Dave started buying more. There was a farmer's market on the mainland that they visited, sitting on the fence between the pens, hoping they would be unnoticed. Of course the local farmers, who all knew each other, immediately recognized them as newcomers and beginners. Embarrassed though they were, they did finally buy more goats.

The first was called Tansy and after her they bought four or five more, trying hard to calculate the right amount for the Community's milk supply. That winter the herd grew to nine goats.

Dave and David learned about goat farming: taking the goat, in season, to the billy goat, seeing the kids born and beginning to milk the nanny. An important step was discovering The Scottish Goat Society. This collection of retired English generals, school heads and 'tweedies' had a common interest in self-sufficiency; it was their entire life, like a religion. The goat business seemed to take over Dave and David's entire life, too.

Through the winter all the household at North College

got used to their routine. Though there was a cold water tap at the barn, hot water had to be carried down from North College. It got dark very early in the evening so they carried a paraffin lamp and milked the goats by its yellow light. Eventually the weather grew so cold that the barn tap froze. They ran out of hay and had to travel to the mainland to buy more for feeding the animals. With animal food in the barn, mice became regular inhabitants so the cats moved down from South College. Solomon and Sheba were brother and sister, born on a farm not too far from Yeldall. They were farm cats really and Sheba was never very domesticated. Soloman was quite affectionate; he seemed to prefer living in the house, but his help in the barn was essential.

The goats were clever, much cleverer than cows. They had personality and could be quite cantankerous. The inside of the barn had been rebuilt, with goat pens made of wood picked up around the farm. There were two little kids in a pen; one would put his head through the bars to hold the gate steady while the other would pull the bolt to let them out. A couple of the goats were happy to jump all kinds of fences, whatever the height.

Having only a small herd of goats, it was possible to get to know them and each had a name, not a number. They would come when their names were called. Then Crystal became ill; it was clear that she would not recover. Dave and David discussed what to do next. They would have to take her to the abattoir. Like the local small farmers they could not have afforded a complete loss, so it was decided that Crystal would be butchered and brought home to eat.

Dave and David loaded her into the van and drove off. Dave had never been to the slaughterhouse before, but David had. Though there were days when the goats were so obstinate and mischievous that David could have killed them himself, they felt like friends. Immediately they arrived Crystal sensed what was happening. She could smell blood, and got nervous. Dave mustered up his courage and suggested they stay with her and go through the whole process. Growing up on a farm, David had found the best thing was to drop the animals off and drive away, ignoring what was happening. But what Dave said made sense, and anyway, there in the pen was Crystal, looking to see if they were with her. As she was moved from pen to pen, she kept looking through the rails, and seeing that they were still there with her, she relaxed.

Crystal died peacefully. As she was electrocuted, they found themselves saying under their breath, 'Lord, bless Crystal'. It was hard being face to face with death, but it was part of life. The men at the slaughterhouse understood their reactions. They said it was hard for all the small farmers when an animal was lost.

Driving home, Dave and David considered how to tell everyone, especially the children, when the meat would be eaten. This was the day for the Eucharist and somehow life and death seemed close. The children from the household, David and Martha Pulkingham, had already found out about Crystal's death, so the Community talked about death and prayed for Crystal during the service.

The farm acquired a billy goat which occupied one of the fields. He was extremely friendly, but he smelled bad. Ironically, his name was Excellence. Excellence's odour was so awful and pervasive that the windows of North College could never be opened. Whoever fed him had to put on a special 'billy goat coat' because Excellence would rush over to greet them and would brush against them; the odour would never come out of their clothes. Poor Excellence. To be so sweet and friendly but so smelly! Everyone felt sorry for him.

Sometimes on Sundays, Dave did not have time to change after feeding the animals before going to the

Eucharist in the Cathedral. He arrived in his old work coat and boots, wrapped up against the cold. But he smelled so badly of Excellence that some would sit on the other side of the Cathedral just to avoid having to give Dave the Peace!

The children enjoyed the farm. Witnessing birth and death was a new experience. Two kids were born and one grew very sick. David was worried; it was a serious loss for even one baby goat to die. The local vets were unable to come over to the island immediately so he bought some glucose hoping the kid would keep it down to get some energy. He decided to stay with it through the night to keep giving it the glucose and to keep it warm. Martha wanted to stay too, despite school the next day. Betty was sceptical about letting her stay up, but was eventually persuaded. They fed the kid through the night, holding it close to keep it warm, and it survived.

It was a bumbling approach to farming, and one that fascinated and amused the local farmers, but they were friendly and ready to offer help and advice. A local man, Robert Hill, lent a hand on the farm from time to time; he had once had a farm of his own. He introduced David and Dave to Jimmy Allen who had a hill farm further north on the island, and a much respected local farmer. Jimmy befriended the two Community men and encouraged them with helpful tips over cups of tea around his kitchen table. The informality and the friendship were signs that with the local farmers, the Community had arrived home.

CHAPTER SEVEN

By the Sweat of Their Brow

SOUTH COLLEGE KITCHEN
Please take care, especially when washing up for the common meals, that pans, serving dishes and utensils are replaced in the correct places, according to the labels on the shelves. This is helpful in keeping the kitchen clean and tidy.

Community Forum Notes, 10th August 1977

SECULAR MUSIC
A performance of rock music by a group from the Community has been indefinitely postponed until issues concerning the verbal message of the songs can be resolved.

Community Forum Notes, 11th October 1977

Seventy-five energetic Fisherfolk musicians, administrators, playwrights, counsellors and teachers could not suddenly lay down their creativity as one would lay down one's guitar at the end of a service. To fill the vacuum from the loss of the travelling ministry, the Fisherfolk experienced a surge of everyday creativity; the bakery staff created new caramel squares, and wholemeal breads; the composers and arrangers in the music business were busy working on new manuscripts; the maintenance division redecorated South College. There was, of course, an ever-expanding menagerie on the farm. Yet all this creativity and intense activity could not fill the significant void which had been the thrill of performance. Strangely enough, it was the maintenance crew who took up their guitars again in an extraordinary way.

South College kitchen was still in constant use; common meals for the whole Community were prepared there. The floor which was made of flagstones was uneven, hard to clean and difficult for constant standing and walking around. David Gustafson drew up plans for the replacement of the floor. The task would involve digging out the old floor with its four-inch-thick flagstones and then another eight inches of rubble and sand. Nine young men from the Community joined David on the work; they estimated one and a half tons of material had to be removed before the new cement foundation could be put in.

David's team worked all day and into the evening for the two weeks it took to clear and redo the floor. The work was usually finished around midnight. One night they decided to spend some maintenance money and go to the pub; they were hot, dusty and dry. The Community had always been cautious about pubs, yet here they found themselves among the local men for whom a drink at the end of a hard day was a way of life. When these Community men went to the pub, they took their guitars with them. They sang Beatles' songs on those late nights.

The children in the Community heard about their elders doing 'rock' music in the pub. But all they had heard themselves were the classical pieces the Community performed with the Choral Society. After a Christmas performance of 'The Messiah', the children asked when the Community would do something they would like musically. The idea was formed and became a production of not just a few songs from the pub, but a performance of the Beatles' 'Sergeant Pepper' album.

The music caught on. As they became more involved in local life through the bakery and the farm, the Fisherfolk wanted more and more to make music. Perhaps it was inevitable that so much musical and creative energy would overflow into local life as the Community dug its roots into island life.

Most of the Community members had grown up on rock and popular music. Many had been at university at the time of riots in the late sixties with huge reactions against the Vietnam war. The disillusionment with society had resulted in their looking for an alternative and to some extent it was for this reason they invested their creative energy in the alternative lifestyle of the Community. In their worship life the Fisherfolk were able to offer their creative talents, the best that they had, to God. But somehow they needed and wanted to make music for its own sake—like the Scots!

The music of a small Scottish community like Millport had its origins in a long history of festivity and carnival. People made music because they wanted to make music and for no other reason. Worship for Celebration was to make the fruits of creativity, music, dance and drama, an offering of their life to God. The Scots gave life to Community of Celebration by bringing to them an opportunity to make music for the joy of it.

The Scottish love of music and the *ceilidh* refreshed and interested everyone. Jimmy Allen told stories of Hogmanay in the old days; of members of the family and strangers alike gathering at 'first-footing' to tell their stories and sing their songs. Some of this tradition had been transferred, in modern terms, to the social gatherings that were a nightly event in the local pubs.

Just behind the Cathedral property, where cars enter and leave by a bumpy cinder track that twists around the Annexe and runs east for fifty yards before sloping steeply into George Street, is the Mansewood Hotel. During the winter, the Fisherfolk began to perform occasionally at the Mansewood, singing contemporary songs. The 'gigs' were successful enough that the following summer they put on several open-air concerts down near the Garrison.

Sandy Hardyman got more involved with the local music. She had befriended Jim and Helen Coyle who owned the Millerston Hotel out to the west of Millport. Dave Porter, Judith Harris, Richard Gullen, Max Dyer and others joined with Sandy to form their own folk group. Conway joined in many of the dramatic presentations that added to the entertainment. Louise, from the branch shop, learned to play Scottish folk music on her fiddle, and then some Scottish folk like Ian Lundie joined in. They performed not only at the Millerston on regular occasions, but also in the town and during the island's festival, Cumbrae Week. They performed both popular and religious songs, anything from jazz to folk and even some Fisherfolk favourites. The local people loved all of it. Music was deep in their blood and Louise's fiddle playing got their feet moving.

Then Jimmy Allen from the hill farm had a fatal heart attack. Having become such firm friends, his death was a sad loss to the farm staff. His wife, whom Dave and David had met many times in the farm kitchen with Jimmy, gave them his animals: geese, hens and ducks. Judith joined Dave and David on the farm and the three of them learned to clip the birds' wings to keep them in the yard.

Charlie was an old and seasoned duck. In fact, he was probably the ugliest duck in creation; his face was gnarled and scratchy and his feathers were falling out. By David's estimation, Charlie's head must have been run over by a truck! Despite being smaller than them, Charlie attacked the geese if they bothered him, and despite his features, he carried himself proudly. He must have been the king duck at some previous residence. Charlie had a mate named Arabella, a bright, young duck.

One morning Judith discovered that Arabella had flown to the top of a telegraph pole and regardless of Charlie's distress stayed up there. She looked down in a supercilious sort of manner, while Charlie moped around—in duck language he was distressed! Eventually Arabella flew away. Charlie was so grief-stricken he would not even eat. Judith was extremely worried about him and kept the household regularly informed on Charlie's progress, or lack of it. Surprisingly, a few days later, Arabella returned and landed in the yard. Her wings were clipped again and she and Charlie got back together.

A batch of geese hatched and rushed around the new yard. Dave thought it would be good for them to have some water and, as there was no pond, he dug a hole and set an old bathtub in it at ground level. Unfortunately once the baby geese were in it, they could not climb out over the slippery sides. No one noticed their plight and they all drowned.

The children helped build a large chicken run and worked on the expanded farm with the somewhat motley crew of workers. However, a previous problem was repeating itself. As before with the 'one goat', there were too few birds to supply eggs for the entire Community. The solution seemed straightforward. If more hens were bought there would be enough eggs for everyone and the Community could stop buying them in the shops.

Extending the chicken pen was a major project. Dave, Judith and David scouted around and found wood to build with and knocked something together. Without any money, they were forced to scour the property and use every bit of old wood that they could find.

At last there were enough chickens to supply eggs to all the households, but the geese would have to go! They were really bad-tempered, attacking anyone who came too close, especially in the laying season. Judith found she had to carry a stick to beat them off, even when she fed them.

Most of what the farm staff had to do was done with little or no equipment. They manured the field, carrying the manure in buckets to spread it out. The vegetables were cultivated by hand and the hay harvested without a machine, using pitchforks to turn the hand-scythed hay.

The local farmers were a quiet lot, but they never missed a thing and knew everything that was going on. They knew when the Community's goats were in season. They knew how many chickens there were. They laughed about the methods saying the Community set farming back twenty years. Yet it became obvious to the local farmers that Dave and David were going to stick at the task, not for show or as a pastime but, like them, to make the farm work and to survive by it. Co-operation and respect grew as well as friendship. Through the next two seasons, Dave and David often helped out on other farms in return for machinery to use on the Cathedral property: a plough for the garden, a muck-spreader or bailer for the fields.

The Community did not make the transition to goat's milk very well. So Dave and David decided to buy cows. They went back to the mainland cattle market and made a helpful contact. John ran a farm that specialized in supplying small farms with animals. Being beginners at farming, neither David nor Dave knew how to look for a good cow. They could have been sold anything. In fact, they bought a small milking Ayrshire. She gave more milk in one day than three goats. A sigh of relief went through the Community as people went back to cow's milk. Milk consumption went right up. One or two people stuck with the goat's milk. 'We committed ourselves to goat's milk and we're going to drink it whether anyone else does or not!' they said.

Dave and David were unsure. Should they change the pattern on the farm? They decided to go back to John and buy another cow, and this one gave four gallons a day. All the milking was being done by hand. Then Tom Lees visited the Community for a while and assisted in buying a milking machine.

Now they were really in business! Having started with just one goat, the farm now had cows, chickens, ducks, goats and a garden. David began to keep the books carefully, checking in all the expenditure to see if the operation was economical and the old community store was re-opened to sell the produce to the Community at cost price.

Self-sufficiency seemed closer. The farm was producing all the milk and eggs that the Community needed. There was leftover bread in constant supply from the bakery and the garden was the main source of vegetables. An added benefit was being close to the earth and close to the changing seasons. The whole Community would turn out to pick up potatoes by hand, trudging through the mud to empty their buckets into waiting sacks. It was back breaking. David realized how much he was enjoying being around the animals, working together with Dave and Judith and all the others who joined them. He didn't even mind the ice, the water and mud.

There was often more milk and left-over bread than the Community could consume, even after Graham Pulkingham had made some delicious goat cheese. The ideal solution seemed to be to build a sty by the barn and get some pigs, 'just a few'. The pigs could be fattened up to the size for butchering and then the Community would also have meat from the farm. As usual, no one had ever worked with pigs before.

When the time arrived to slaughter the first pigs, Dave and David backed their old yellow van down the track to the gateway to the farmyard. Dave placed an old door in position as a ramp, but there were no sides. He then began to herd the pigs onto the ramp. They jumped off the sides, squealing and kicking up the mud. Not all of them got clean away. Dave managed to grab one and David turned around in time to see him holding on for dear life and being dragged, flat-out, through the cold, wet mud. The more they were chased, the more the pigs went crazy and ran.

There was lots of help. The farm had been planned as an area of Community life in which guests could be involved. It was hard sometimes to tell whether the guests were going to be a help or a hindrance. Many people came to the Community for pastoral care, their lives in disorder. They could work on the farm, but not the bakery where considerable skill was necessary.

Some really clever and theological guests arrived; they wanted to spend their time leaning on their tools and talking about the important and deep theological questions of life, like the meaning and purpose of community. The Community workers had hardly enough time. There was so much to do in the summer that they could only just get everything done and still attend the worship services in the Cathedral. A policy was instituted that such heavy talking could only occur during the tea breaks.

There were some guests who needed a lot of help. One man arrived who was so distressed he was unaware of what he was doing. He set out to rake the grass cuttings from the lawn. When David went over later, the grass was scattered everywhere. There was no system, no line of raked grass, no heap of cuttings.

David bought fruit bushes, currants and gooseberries, and planted them at the southern end of the vegetable garden near the orchard. The garden was well-planned and in the autumn they had cleared some ground for the new bushes. These were small but growing well. An enthusiastic guest appeared who seemed quite competent. David sent him down to weed around the garden. Shortly after, the guest appeared. 'I've finished; look down there.' The guest had taken a scythe and laid the weeds low. David could not believe his eyes—where had all the fruit bushes gone? Surely they were a little to the left of where the man had been working. As David walked closer, he knew the truth. He resisted the terrible temptation to strangle the man.

'You didn't happen to see any fruit bushes down here, did you?'

'Uh . . . . no . . . . were there bushes down here?'

David told him as quietly as he could manage. . . .

Mimi came out of South College one morning to find some rather rough-looking children throwing stones at the ducks. It was the school holidays and these Glasgow children were staying on the island.

She called out to them, 'Stop doing that!' They jumped, somewhat alarmed and poised to run. Mimi continued, 'If you come back tomorrow, I'll get Judith to give you a tour of the whole farm, to see all the animals.'

They did come back. One boy named James made a special friendship with Judith and came every day that summer. His dad was part of a Glasgow gang and the boy was not missed as he worked on the farm all day. So many children liked coming to the farm that eventually, in order to get the work done, Dave and David had to find a system. David organized all the workers and Dave took time to chat and jolly them along. He had the patience for them. There were six to eight children every time, children like James who were often in trouble and didn't fit in anywhere socially. One was hyperactive, but the pace of the farm suited him and there wasn't too much difficulty.

Then change came to the farm. Judith planned to move with her household to the States. David got appendicitis and was extremely ill for a long time. Until then Dave and

David had run the kitchen in North College as well as the farm. Now with Dave on his own something had to change.

Douglas and Christine McDavid had lived on Cumbrae for their whole lives. Douglas had met Community members through his job at the gas works where the Community bought its coke but he hadn't got to know them well. Christine was aware of the differences between the town and the Community. Most difficult were the times when something happened at the Cathedral and the town did not know about it. Millport likes to know what is going on. For a while Christine and Douglas ran the holiday home and met the Community when they wanted to use it for rehearsals. Her first impression was of noisy Americans. But she met Sandy who had been a Guide and the Millport Guides needed help with their music. There was a joint concert for the Queen's Jubilee and the Guide leaders invited Sandy in to help. Quite by chance, Christine mentioned that she had always wanted to learn the guitar and Sandy immediately offered to teach her. Sandy helped Christine buy the right guitar, began teaching her, and they fast became friends.

Out of curiosity at first, Christine went to the Community's worship. There the fellowship among the worshippers was warm and encouraging and as time went on she wanted to belong to this family. When there in the midst of the worship she felt refreshed and alive. There were family Eucharists followed by dinner in the Common Room of South College. Eventually Douglas and the children came to Eucharist and the meal, and the whole family made friends with the Community and worshipped regularly at the Cathedral. For Douglas, Sunday morning in the Cathedral was the high point of the week and he never missed a service.

While Christine was pregnant she slipped and fell, hitting her shoulder and causing extreme pain. She could not sleep in bed and for two weeks she sat in a chair to sleep. The doctor allowed her no medicine for the pain and would not X-ray her because of the pregnancy. Ruth Wieting prayed for Christine at the Friday evening healing service and again at the Sunday morning Eucharist.

Christine was also worried about Douglas, whose job was finishing with the closing of the gas works. They went down to George Street for lunch and discussed the possibility of Douglas working on the farm. While Bill and Douglas talked, Christine fell asleep in her chair. When she woke, her shoulder was healed and it seemed that Bill and Douglas had reached an agreement about the farm. Douglas would take over as the new manager.

Jodi organized the guests so they worked for Douglas through the summer along with Sandra Grimes who was there to consider whether God was calling her to the Community permanently. The children still came to work with Douglas and Sandra. Three boys came from a youth opportunity programme. Once they got used to the routine and the steady pace of the farming, they stayed for quite a while till they found more permanent work.

Eventually Christine considered becoming a member at the Cathedral. She questioned whether the idea of her membership at the Cathedral was dependent on the Community or whether it was more than that. God had really done something that renewed everyone in the Cathedral congregation. She could see that he had. But in sorting out her thoughts and feelings, Christine also realized she had become so involved with the Community that she had begun to neglect her longer standing acquaintances and links in the town. For a while it was necessary to re-establish old friendships, to balance the two, so that she could belong to both the town and the Cathedral. Christine was confirmed along with other members of the Cathedral congregation.

CHAPTER EIGHT

Three Movements of the Spirit in this Age

Having come in the summer when no-one has time to do anything except 'Awake, awake to love and work' with a rather excessive emphasis on the work end of the deal. . . . I simply ask what people think of the necessity of spending some time with the Lord. Not to do anything, not to be more effective in your work, just to be together with him. . . .

Letter from Louis Newton to Community AGM October 1978

To have a morning to catch up with your socks—whether washing or darning—is divine

Brother Roland, 19th September 1977

The withdrawal of the flower in Jodi's vision had been interpreted as a corporate, community retreat from public ministry. No one had anticipated that God might also be speaking to individual members of the Community about retreat. But God was about to do something new, something strange and wonderful to the Community. For some, the trip to Detroit was to have been a turning point, not in the ministry of the Community, but in the spirituality of its members. As with so many major changes, God gave them signs.

A bishop from the Detroit area was talking to Graham and listening to the news of the Community in Scotland.

He commented, 'That sounds very good for a two-legged stool. . . .' Graham questioned him further. The bishop said, 'I don't see the place in your Community's life for silence, prayer and contemplation. Any religious community that does not have that firmly in its life cannot exist, except for perhaps one generation. It will not endure without this third aspect.' Graham took the words to heart, bringing the question to the Community.

At home, everyone was extremely busy. The farm and the music business employed nearly all the Community members. The new bakery staff were in the process of being trained in preparation for the take-over. And worship, particularly worship leadership, took up most of the remainder of everyone's time.

On one evening of the week the choir met. Almost all the adults and some of the teenagers were in the choir which was led by Betty and Mimi. Not only was music rehearsed for both the Community's worship and Cathedral services, but new music was being composed for other occasions. Betty, Jodi and others were writing Communion settings and other service music. Lindsay Treen spent long hours copying the manuscripts to have new scores for the choir members. Betty wrote a setting of 'The Magnificat', and named the tune 'Cathedral of the Isles', specifically for Evening Prayer which had become part of the Community's worship schedule. That text and tune have since been incorporated into the new hymnal for the Episcopal Church in the United States. The choir had become a very important part of the worship life of the Community.

The Community Eucharist was held on another evening. Everyone came, along with lots of visitors. It was the focus of teaching and sharing in the life of the Community. The ordinariness of working life and hard days were brought before God and his life was celebrated. People shook off their tiredness and discouragement, offering and being drawn to praise and worship. There was a powerful sense of God's presence. Those who came worn and weary could offer their weariness alongside those who came with joy; together they worshipped in the presence of God. Hearts and bodies were healed. The bread and wine were the presence of Christ and, by his Spirit, imparted the grace for life and the empowering for ministry.

Could it be that in all this activity there was indeed a missing element? Was the third leg missing? The Community could only just sense that this was a word from God. They could not see a way ahead. An active and seemingly tireless drive to establish life was common to everyone. But to find contemplation individually would require a special gift to be established in the Community's life. It perhaps required a very particular ministry, a personalized ministry.

Before the Community had arrived at the Cathedral, at least one of the gifts had been resident on the property. Each year Roland Walls had spent a month in the spring and another in the autumn in retreat in the Monks' Huts. Each hut is about the size of a small garden shed, about six feet long and six feet wide with a low gabled roof; there was a small window in one side wall. The huts were clustered on a small clearing. Three huts faced the centre of the clearing and tracks had been worn between them. One of the monks had laid some pieces of flagstone to make a firmer path. Up a bank at one side of the clearing and behind a line of rhododendron bushes ran the path from South College to George Street. When plans had been made for the Community of Celebration to reside in the Cathedral the monks moved from the huts to a tiny cottage in George Street, but the huts remained.

There had been an early conversation between Roland and the Community. Settled as the Community of the Transfiguration was, the Community of Celebration did not think they were well established. Their rule did not allow them to make any plans for the future! Celebration was full of plans and activity. That was just the point. To Roland it seemed that he and his fellow monks were like a little rubber dinghy bobbing in the bay when along came this huge ocean going tanker called the Community of Celebration, turning the gentle waves to Pacific rollers in its wake. While they had lots in common, the differences were too great for any constructive conversation to take place immediately.

A theological student who spent time visiting the Community of Celebration also studied under Roland in Edinburgh. When he was in Cumbrae he would say, 'Now, have you met Roland Walls yet? The man is a saint, and has incredible wisdom and understanding and you must get to know him.' At Roslin he used to say to Roland, 'Now have you met the Community of Celebration because they are a marvellous group of people. You really must get together.'

Not long after Graham's conversation with the bishop in Detroit, Roland decided he must do something to build a bridge between the two groups. He walked up to the Cathedral and found Graham at home; they had tea together, and now were able to understand each other.

Graham invited Roland to speak to the whole Community. Roland looked around the Common Room. The room, about thirty feet long, faced out towards the west, overlooking the Cathedral entrance. Huge old furniture was carefully placed and the walls opposite the windows were lined with shelves filled with ancient books. The wood panelling and the heavy antique furniture gave a more sombre tone than that of the group who now gathered to meet Roland. People sat in every available space.

As Roland sat down he said, 'I think this is an absolutely remarkable group of people.' They were warming to him already, encouraged that this man with the reputation for being a giant of the faith should think them remarkable.

'Do you know why?' he continued.

They thought, 'Is it because of our worship life, because of our theological understanding, or what?'

Roland turned to Graham and pointing at him said, 'Because you have been able to live with this appalling man all these years!'

He brought the house down because, of course, to live and work with a prophet like Graham can be hard work indeed!

Roland said there are three aspects of the movement of the Spirit in this age. The first is celebration: the body of Christ coming together in a celebration of the joy of the redeemed community. Then there is involvement: the relationship of the redeemed community to the world, working out in daily life how to live 'in the world and not be of the world'. Lastly there is contemplation: solitude 'on one's own-ness'. Discernment is necessary to know the relationship of solitude to Community.

Roland went on to talk about the central but often the most neglected aspect of silence and prayer in a community's life. Each person must make space in their lives for time with God. This would take time and reflection to understand, Roland went on to explain, because it was something more than a ten-minute quiet-time or grace before meals, or even considered intercession. To busy, programme-oriented, ministry-oriented western culture this may seem like a waste of time, a relic from another age. It meant a life of prayer, of a living consciousness of God, of an inner stillness in which to listen to God.

There was a strong, positive response among those gathered. A pilgrimage was begun, one that was to put the third leg on the stool.

Pat Allen, who worked in the bakery branch shop and

lived in a tiny flat above the bakery, came from a Southern Baptist background in the United States. Everything about contemplation was new to her. During an extended visit with Rick and Leslie Roberts and Jerry Barker to Malabar, Australia, the significance of contemplation and of solitude with God deepened in Pat. The idea was, for her, a conversion that was to cause a profound change in her lifestyle, moving her to serve God in a new way. Pat recognized God's voice in Roland's concern for contemplation and retreat.

Members of the Community of Celebration were always available to work anywhere, to go anywhere, to do whatever chores were necessary, and, most of all, to offer their gifts and talents to the corporate life of the Community whenever needed. Pat was one of those with many talents whose gifts were invaluable and irreplaceable. She had been on Fisherfolk teams since she had arrived in Coventry in 1973. She was a pianist and singer, and wrote songs for worship. In Cumbrae she was a key musician for choir and worship services, and she was in constant demand for piano lessons. As a member of the bakery staff, Pat was known well and trusted by the local people. She was outgoing and friendly. Her pastoral skills were recognized by members of the Community who had come to trust her and depend on their time with her. Yet she felt God was calling her to prayer and a life of solitude. Neither Pat nor the Community knew what this would mean for her practically.

In the beginning, she set up a quiet room in her house, and eventually moved it to the South College. The quiet room was a comfortable place, with a huge beanbag chair and floor cushions. A shelf filled with books, on contemplation and prayer, and many more on various aspects of spirituality, sexuality, dreams, inner healing and the lives of the saints and mystics was collected. Pictures, plants, and seashells were lovingly placed about the room, and often there were fresh flowers. A kettle and drinks were provided and a fire and blankets were on hand. The whole atmosphere said, 'Come and stay, for a bit, for as long as you want.'

Different people had previously worked out a variety of prayer disciplines for themselves. But now the Community embraced the idea of a 'quiet day'. Once a month a person could take a complete day when there were no other demands on them and time could be spent alone with God. Depending on the need, work schedules were altered, children were looked after by someone else, and household chores postponed. It became acceptable to choose time alone and apart without waiting for the pressure of 'I feel I am at breaking point. I must have some time off.' Retreat days were not just for the weak or the broken but were becoming a priority and in order for everyone.

Individuals came to the room and Pat helped them through their quiet day, providing a meal, seeing they had a sense of direction in their day, and praying or counselling with those who desired it. One could walk or paint, or simply relax and read.

In these days apart, members became aware of their own sense of self-importance. The travelling schedules of ministry and the intense production schedules in the businesses resulted in feelings that 'everything depends on me' and that 'I am doing marvellous things for God'. In these retreats, as they left their tasks even for just a day, they discovered the world can get on without ministry and busy schedules. In the quietness there is God.

As this third leg was fitted to the Community's stool, Roland was given the authority and freedom to guide and help Pat in her calling. He was aware of God speaking to Pat, particularly as this was such a contrast to her background; a Baptist, and a member of a very active and family-oriented community. Soon she began to take very long retreats of a month at a time. As her calling developed, ways were found to release Pat to live on her own and be freed from other responsibilities and intrusions.

Many in the Community felt hurt as Pat withdrew from the centre of activity. While acknowledging Pat's call from God, it took her away from places where work was still to be done. At times there was great misunderstanding, and as she gradually increased her times of retreat, communication which could have resolved the conflict and growing difficulty was impossible. The children loved Pat and she loved them. They were unable to understand why she had to go away, and why they could not see her and have lessons with her any more. The local people who knew Pat well inquired after her. If she was seen, she just popped into a shop but never stopped to chat as she had done in the past. Marlyn Lundie and Martha Barker began doing shopping for her.

The retreat periods lengthened to virtual solitude. Both Pat and the Community came face to face with what Roland described as a kind of death. Someone loved is suddenly inaccessible. The Pat that they had known—sociable and caring, supporting people in their own solitude, talking with them, encouraging them in their walk with God—was no longer with them. Roland talked with the Community to help them understand Pat and their own feelings and reactions to what was happening.

He talked of death. He said that Pat was following a path that many others had followed safely. She was coming to terms with personal inner darkness, and with the guidance of an experienced spiritual director she would fulfil her calling. It was not just something that she was doing that would give her a pleasant burst of spiritual energy. It was a death. After the death, Roland said, there would be resurrection and glory. But first there would be the pain and sorrow of the loss; while that is happening there is no sign of the glory. He kept saying to the Community, 'Let her die. Let the seed go into the ground and die.' This was the perfect metaphor of the contemplative life. But Roland saw the Community keep trying to pull up the seedling to check that it was all right and still growing. His counsel was that they should leave it and have faith in God to work out Pat's life.

Roland's words, though hard, rang true. When Pat decided finally to move to one of the Monks' Huts permanently, the Community was ready to help. The huts were hidden amidst the foliage and in the spring snowdrops and bluebells flourished among narrow paths between the overhanging trees. They were isolated enough from the outside world, while at the same time accessible and in safe proximity to the South College. Dave Porter cleared undergrowth and began to make a beautiful place. A grill was erected for outdoor cooking, and a tiny stove was purchased for cooking meals in one hut. A cable was laid from South College to supply electricity to heat the huts against the bitter cold of winter and a room in South College was left free in case Pat found she needed it.

The Community felt protective towards Pat as she moved to live in these simple surroundings. They feared she would be too cold or would be at risk if someone should wander through the woods and disturb her at night. One stormy night Jodi lay awake and found herself praying for Pat's safety. Eventually she fell asleep. In the morning it was easy to see why the Lord had woken her. A tree, uprooted by the storm, had only just been prevented from falling on the huts by catching in the branches of two other trees. Pat was safe.

Pat Allen was a constant, though silent, reminder of the love and care of God for his people. On the notice board in the cloister next to the household post boxes was a square labelled 'Hermit's Corner'. It continued to be her link with the Community. She would place bits of her poetry there, letters, quotations, or reassuring bits of scripture, all of which were an encouragement and blessing to the Community. One extract said:

> One Word
>   spake the Father
> which Word
>   was his son
> and this Word
>   he speaks ever
> in eternal silence
>   and in silence
> must it be heard
>   by the soul
>
> Saint John of the Cross

The seed which God planted in the midst of the Community was surely growing.

CHAPTER NINE

On the Basis of Kingdom Principles

....the new theological training programme....is open to (male) Community members. (Graham explained that.... women might well be able to be involved, although not as candidates for ordination.)

Community Forum Notes 6th September 1978

The Community held an annual meeting every January to review their life. At one such meeting some members shared the frustration that they had felt for several years in their personal lack of theological understanding of the Community's life. Many had dropped out of college years before and few had any theological training. Was the Community of Celebration a unique happening in the history of the church? Was there a theological basis for the type of community that had come into being? All wanted a deeper understanding of the history of community in different ages and cultures. There was a deep wish to grasp more firmly the traditions by which the church had been nurtured and to understand Christians of different denominations. Those who travelled on Fisherfolk ministry were particularly aware of their lack of theological training. They had encountered interpretations of scripture and of worship they could not agree with, but were unable to address adequately. In their ignorance they seemed to be walking through theological minefields. When Graham travelled with them he provided the necessary understanding. But the Community knew that others should understand the theological perspective of their life, not only for their own sake, but for their ministry within the church.

Roland offered both to help design a theological course for the Community and to be the tutor. Together he and the Community decided that he would teach a small group who would be able then to teach the rest of the Community. Roland planned a three-year course of two terms each year. These fitted around the summer schedules of the bakery so the terms were spring and autumn, times when Roland customarily visited the island on retreat.

Working on church history, biblical theology and Bible study, the group studied set books. These were discussed in weekly seminars. The programme was not an attempt to produce academic theologians, but rather to enable the group to reflect on their own experience of God, to understand the theology of their experience.

For some, education in the past had been particularly negative and only over the first term were they able to realize that studying need not be competitive. No one had to show their cleverness; understanding was for the benefit of everyone. If anyone failed to work they impoverished the rest of the group because everyone's contribution was a vital part of the process.

To the Community members the study was a considerable effort. For Roland it was a sacrificial offering as he gave up a lot of the time that he normally spent in solitude. Those who were on the course had the Bishop's permission to preach in the Cathedral, an extension of Bob's responsibility to other Community members. Most were not considering becoming ordained but recognized the need for theologically educated lay people.

Roland's ecumenical perspective influenced the Community's relationship with Millport. There were four denominations present in the churches on the island, Brethren, Roman Catholic, Church of Scotland and the Cathedral. Roland worshipped with each of these congregations. He helped the Community to analyse and understand its theology of worship, to broaden it, and then reminded them to take their worship resources to the other churches. Bill, Mimi and Jackie volunteered to be on the rota to play the organ at the Church of Scotland. Several took their guitars down to the Catholic Church on special occasions. It was not Roland's desire that the Community change; he only hoped that he might be part of the process that would enrich what they already had.

And as he did with Pat Allen, Roland helped a number of people through times of crisis or changes of direction.

Roland caused the Community of Celebration, poor though they thought they were, to look beyond themselves to the poor of Scotland who had none of the choices and advantages of the Community. His contact with the wayfarers and tramps who called on him was a constant sign of his concern, and he was sure to point out the biblical texts concerning the poor, texts which the Community might otherwise have overlooked.

The Isle of Cumbrae lay close to the mouth of the Clyde. Away to the north and west a great channel of water separated the island from Kintyre. Across the narrow channel just south of Largs and directly across from Millport there was a power station—nuclear power. The plant was extended to four times its original size till at night its brightness shone across the water like a scene from a science fiction film. Friends from Sweden who were visiting asked the Community if the islanders had been given pills to take for radiation sickness. No one in the Community had even thought about it before. The Swedes went on to surmise that if there was an accident, Millport would be devastated. No. There were no pills and no plans to evacuate islanders to safety. The Community began to recognize their own powerlessness. They were people forgotten by those with power and money in the south in Whitehall. People in power did not care too much that something awful might happen way off the coast of Scotland.

There was a major weapons stockpile just up the coast but there was a more visible reminder of the nuclear threat. Polaris submarines had their base in the Clyde, slipping up and down the deep channel on their various missions. In the summertime when the weather was fine and sunny, the black hulls could be seen lying in the channel out to the west of Cumbrae practising emergency routines. The submarines surfaced and the crews leapt out onto life rafts. Those most obvious were the practice ones not carrying nuclear warheads, but to observers on the island there was no difference between one submarine and another. They might all be carrying weapons. To see and consider the lethal potential of each submarine left Community members stunned.

Concern about war had always been part of the Community's life. Back in the days in Houston many of the young men in the Church of the Redeemer had been liable to be drafted and sent to Vietnam. Bill became a conscientious objector, refusing 'on the basis of Kingdom principles'. Graham, as Rector of the Church, wrote to the Draft Board explaining those principles and eventually Bill was allowed to do his service at the Church. The move to England had temporarily put such concerns to one side in favour of involvement in the mushrooming charismatic renewal.

On one of his visits to the United States shortly after the

move to Scotland, Graham again met Jim Wallis and other members of Sojourners Community from Washington. This was a socially active group looking for some help in stabilizing their community's pastoral life; for this they visited Houston.

Several significant forces for renewal began in the '60s. There was interest in God and Eastern religions. There was an enormous youth reaction against the war in Vietnam. There was charismatic renewal and there was a movement for justice at the local level. These had been unable to mix and often the groups involved were suspicious of one another. Graham, while recognizing the time was right for seeking spiritual renewal within the charismatic movement, never lost sight of the concern for peace and justice. In meeting Jim Wallis and Bob and Jackie Sabath, he saw the coming together of two aspects that were equally crucial to him. There was now opportunity for the marriage between pastoral and prophetic; pastoral expressing the care for each and every person in their walk with God and the life of the church; and prophetic taking God's life into the world. For a time the Sojourner's magazine nurtured the Community's interest in the gospel principles of peace and justice.

The Community started two study groups, one following Ronald Sider's book, *Rich Christians in an Age of Hunger*. The other group read about nuclear weapons and nuclear power. The study resulted in action. Some members of the Community joined a march at a nuclear power station near Edinburgh.

Demonstrations usually happened at weekends, but if the bakery was not too busy people were able to be set free from work. There was a CND rally, walking to Faslane with a crowd of thousands. People from the Iona Community were there too. As the crowd collected outside the gates of the base, those inside hung out of their windows to taunt and jeer at them. Participation in this and other peace demonstrations helped the Community understand the depth of feeling surrounding these issues, not only for those opposed, but for those who were employed in the nuclear industry and depended on its expansion for their livelihood. Christians from the U.S. Navy submarine base visited the Community of Celebration and talked of their work. Both the Community and these young sailors found encouragement to be faithful and to trust in God for guidance and safety.

As they studied the issues and travelled to marches in Scotland, the Community met many like-minded people. Donald Scott and Leslie Reid were friends of the Kenmuir Street Community in Glasgow. Kenmuir is a 'close' community; its loose-knit membership live in or near a Scottish close on Kenmuir Street, and all give their time and energy to the needs of that neighbourhood. Donald and Leslie, both social workers in Edinburgh, visited the Community of Celebration many times, sharing their concerns and bringing to the quietness of Cumbrae the problems of the inner-city. They learned a lot from one another, and eventually, with Alan Kreider of the London Mennonite Centre and Mike Sweatman from Edinburgh, collaborated on the book, *Time to Choose*, a study book that the Community published on the nuclear issue. The response, from friends in various parts of Britain, was sufficient for the Community to include conferences on these issues as part of their newly developing conference ministry.

Roland insisted on making the connection between the gospel, pastoral life, and justice and peace. The small theological study group looked at the scriptures, the history of the church, and contemporary life. There was constant dialogue about what was being studied and the group's understanding of history being shaped in the present day, both in the Community's pastoral and worship life and in the world around them.

The Community began to take notice of what till then had been to them an obscure festival on the church's calendar, the Feast of the Transfiguration. Roland had been teaching on the poor, beginning by pointing out a connection between the Feast of the Transfiguration and his own Community's name; the feast is a focal point for their life. The day the atomic bomb was dropped on Hiroshima was the same day as the Church's Feast of the Transfiguration. The two stand in opposition to one another, a great irony that cannot be ignored. Martha Barker suddenly realized the stark truth which she was facing. She wrote about it:

TRANSFIGURATION

'*Now there are only two radiations we move toward: the radiation of Christ or the radiation of the atom.*'

Brother Roland Walls

August 6 Feast of Transfiguration

Behold the Christ
the mountain vision
radiating the splendour of God
revealing the potential of humanity.
Behold the radiant God man:
fulfilment of Moses' law
fulfilment of Elijah's prophecy.
Behold, O man
and be struck dumb
by unspeakable glory.
On the mountain—
humanity glorified
but in the valley
humanity writhes
in the wasted shape

of the small boy
by dumb demons driven.

Transfiguration's mountain vision
is robed in human flesh
as the radiant Jesus descends
touches the twisted shape,
driving tormentors away,
restoring humanity's glory
completing transfiguration.

August 6 Feast of Disfiguration

Behold Nagasaki, Hiroshima
their mountains splendid
with atomic fire
their peoples transfigured
by atomic blast,
their survivors
writhing in the valley
begging some splendid Christ
to touch and make whole.

Behold the radiant Bomb:
defying the law
ignoring the prophets.
Behold, O man
and be struck dumb
by unspeakable terror.

Feast
of Disfiguration
born not of the mountain's vision
but of dumb demons
refusing to see in other—
sister and brother
seeing only
enemy
building always walls

to keep the other out:
Democracy/Communism
Black/White
Male/Female
Rich/Poor
Christian/Muslim
build the walls
behind them pile defences
enough to obliterate the other
before they obliterate us,
until some jumpy finger
in a moment of dumb
panic
pushes the button
and the smoking timbers
of our civilised lives
lie charred heaps
against the fouled sky.

August 6 Feast of Transfiguration/Feast of Disfiguration

'Now there are only two ways to walk:
Toward the radiance of the transfigured Christ
or the radiance of the Bomb.'

Toward the radiance that descends
to touch, to heal, to restore
or
toward the radiance that descends
to defend, to murder, to destroy.

Toward the radiance that glorifies,
or the radiance that vaporises.

'This day I set before you life and death,
a blessing and a curse:
Choose this day
whom you will serve.'

Martha Keys Barker (2 August 1980)

Choices were being made in Britain and by the rest of the world and they were clear choices. The Community of Celebration began to celebrate the Feast with reference to Hiroshima. Cathleen used Japanese brush painting to produce scenes of the transfiguration of Christ and of Hiroshima. The children learned about it. The Feast stayed in the consciousness and affected preaching, worship and prayer at other times because it was in people's hearts and minds.

The word of God was being applied more broadly than in their own parochial setting. Cathleen spent time with the children to teach them about intercession and to hear about things around them that were worrying. On television they saw news of events around the world. There were newspaper headlines and conversations at the meal tables. The children began to pray in the household and in the Community's worship for the poor and politically oppressed. Those leading prayers in services began including photos and pictures the children brought. The children adopted particular concerns for prayer. Stephanie began to pray for local old people; Luke prayed for Japan and Clare for the United States. Michelle prayed for Poland and an orphan boy named Fadi from Lebanon. Hannah prayed for the lonely.

The children took their own initiative and organized a 'bring-and-buy' sale in the back garden of the household where Clare and Hannah Morris lived. Clare and Hannah, Zoe, Stephanie and Christopher McKeown collected up their own toys and encouraged their friends and neighbours to come and buy. A notice was made to stick on the wall for passers-by to see. There were announcements in the Community forum and posters on the notice board. A table was set out in the garden and the children waited rather excitedly for 'opening time'. The sale raised seven pounds which was sent off to Oxfam with a letter carefully written by Clare and signed by all of them.

Some households gave money over and above their regular tithe to Oxfam and Christian Aid, consciously changing their eating habits to save the money. For a while there was a 'Coffee Day', the only day in the week when coffee was available. On the other days there was hot water if anyone wanted it.

It was a process, a direction. The Community never declared itself pacifist or proclaimed a defined position and continued to have members of every sort of political persuasion. The study process was one of reflection and growth, bringing change and varying viewpoints. They understood that all positions had some measure of validity, and all positions could and would eventually change.

CHAPTER TEN

In the Presence of God

Worship and teaching services have continued through the summer, and have been attended by many visitors as well as Community. There have also been many guests at the Thursday evening family eucharist and meal.

Newsletter August/September 1980

Nan and Bill Cunningham had regularly taken their holidays on the Isle of Cumbrae. They came down from Glasgow with their three children, Lesley, Gillian and Gary, and hired a caravan on the local site. One evening Nan was walking back home to the site from the town but was distracted by the notice board that announced a regular eight o'clock service in the Cathedral. She went up the path and gently opened the door. She had stumbled on a choir practice; the service was eight in the morning not the evening. Sitting quietly at the back of the Cathedral, Nan found herself in tears, very moved by the sounds, the music and the atmosphere. No one approached her and as the music came to an end she crept out and went home.

On Friday evening Nan came back, for the Community were leading special services for the summer season. Since neither the priest nor the preacher, Graham, were wearing dog-collars, Nan could only reflect that here was an ordinary man from the congregation preaching. He kept asking, 'Are you listening, are you following me?' Nan was listening and following, for God was touching her deeply. Bill and Mimi came over and spoke to her when the service was over.

The following morning, the end of their holiday, the Cunningham family returned to Glasgow. Nan told the people in her local church how she had been so affected by the worship at the Cathedral, but Bill was not interested. He was extremely anti-church.

March came around the following year and Nan raised the subject of booking the caravan for this year's holiday in Millport. Bill laughed. 'We have no money and some large bills to pay. There's no way we can have a holiday this year.'

Nan was not to be put off easily. 'Then I'll get a job!' she said.

'You must be joking. Everyone's out of work and you think you'll get a job?'

'I am going to try.'

'And who do you think will give you a job for twelve weeks?' It was twelve weeks to Bill's holiday from his work.

Nan was not so easily deterred. The worship had brought her close to God with fresh power and revitalized her sense of hope. The Spirit had been at work to bring her to the Cathedral and she was absolutely sure her family must go back to the island. Before she went to sleep, Nan had decided that she would go to the Job Centre where she would find the means to get her family back to Millport. And before she dropped off to sleep, Nan prayed.

The next morning Nan was up and dressed in her smartest outfit and as soon as the children went off to school she caught the bus into the town. The Job Centre looked depressing. Nan was not sure if her hopes were raised in vain. She went over to the counter and explained that she was looking for a job and told the man what she could do.

The man shook his head apologetically. 'There is one job here that you could do, but I'm sure it is not what you are looking for. It is only a temporary job lasting twelve weeks.' Nan could have hugged him—only for twelve weeks indeed! She knew it had been the Lord and thanked him all the way home, knowing that he had given them the money to go on holiday.

When they arrived in Millport, Nan went up to the Cathedral to check on the service times. While she was there, Alison Barker invited the Cunningham family to the Community Eucharist and to the supper which followed. Nan told her that there was no way that Bill would come because he never set foot in the church, but she and the children would be pleased to accept.

She decided to try anyway. He said an emphatic no, but she went on to explain, 'Bill, it's a family service with a meal together afterwards. They're expecting us and they're going to feed us and the kids.' This was a different matter and in the end Bill agreed.

The Common Room was packed for the informal midweek Eucharist and as they entered, Bill and Nan got separated in the crowd. She was worried but then surprised when she spotted him, for he was singing.

For the remainder of their stay in Millport, everywhere Bill and Nan went in the town they ran into Community people who recognized them. 'Hello, Bill, how are you?' 'Hi, Bill, how's the holiday?' No matter where they went, there was the Community treating them as friends. Nan began to suspect that God was being quite active in Bill's life.

On their last evening, a Friday, a friend who was a

minister from Glasgow came to join them, to give the Cunninghams a ride back into Glasgow. Malcolm suggested they pray together. Bill knew something was going to happen to him. As he sensed there was no way to control the feeling, he was afraid. It was as if the Lord had taken him by the scruff of his neck and said, 'This is what church is to be; this is Christianity, not what you expected and not what you've experienced before.' Among these Christians Bill had experienced a God who was real; to be with them in their worship was to be in the presence of God. Bill knew he had to decide to say 'yes' or 'no' to God. There was no longer a way to ignore him or even to reason that God might not be real or might not be concerned with ordinary working people.

Bill looked at the faces of the others in the dim light of the caravan. These were his friends and his wife, people who loved him, with whom he belonged. They shared with him their experience of God and how they had given their lives to Jesus.

In a rush of words and a flood of tears, Bill asked Jesus to come into his life and to be his Saviour. As they prayed for themselves and for Bill, the others cried too.

Back home in Glasgow, life continued much the same as ever. Bill had experienced something different with the Community and wanted the church in Glasgow to change. But it was the same, and both he and Nan wanted more. Together they prayed for some sign from God of what they should do next.

The couple who ran the caravan site in Millport chose to call in that evening to bring some things the Cunninghams had left in the caravan the previous summer. It soon became apparent that this couple were Christians. Nan and Bill talked of the Cathedral people and how much they wanted to be with them. The man had lots of friends and contacts on the island and offered to help Bill find a job in Millport. Perhaps the family should move there?

Nan and Bill talked over the idea after the couple had left. Was it really possible to move to the island? They wanted eventually to become members of the Community and had even talked to Bill Farra about the possibility. If Bill were able to work on the island with the family living in Millport, they could have more contact with the Community and discuss possible membership. At least they would be close. They prayed together.

Bill phoned the estate agents on Cumbrae the following day. The family had only their savings of ten thousand pounds; Bill knew they would be unable to get a mortgage as he would probably not be earning much. Strangely enough, a house had come onto the market just hours before at ten thousand pounds. The Cunninghams viewed it the following Sunday. Although it was a tiny one-bedroom flat, they loved it. A friend, a surveyor looked at the flat for them; within days their offer was accepted and they became the owners. The Lord seemed to be giving more than signs: he was opening doors.

During the time from the holiday and through to the purchasing of the flat the Cunninghams had talked to the Community of Celebration about becoming members. While they were very keen on the family coming to Millport to consider joining the Community, there was hesitation on the part of the Community over whether or not it was the right time. They suggested that Nan and Bill and their children should live and work in Millport, becoming a bridge between the Community and the town. The adjustment for a family coming from Glasgow to the tiny island community would take a lot of effort, without the added pressure of going from ordinary family life into a Community household. To the Cunninghams it seemed a very painful rejection. They thought of all that God had done to bring them there and now the Community were saying, 'No, not yet.'

They were marooned, away from their families and friends in Glasgow and not yet belonging to the new family.

Bill was unemployed for seven months until finally he got a job with the Hydro-Board. After a year in Millport, Bill and Nan began to ask themselves about their house. The children were growing up fast and it was hard to manage in such a small place with all of them so cramped together. The lack of a permanent job meant that no building society would consider a mortgage for the purchase of the derelict flat below theirs to convert the two into one larger flat. They asked the Community for advice, and Bill Farra offered Bill a permanent job in the bakery in order that he would be able to secure the mortgage. Bill handed in his notice to the Hydro-Board.

One afternoon while still working out his notice with the Hydro-Board Bill was alone digging a ditch to lay an electric cable, when he began to feel a pain in his chest. He stopped digging for a while and the pain subsided. He started to work again, but so did the pain. He decided that when he had finished work, he would see the doctor. It was an unusual pain, one that he had never experienced before. Bill took a break and had his lunch, then got back to digging. Then the pain began again, but the gaps between times of the pain being there, coming again and again, were getting less. He decided to rest a few minutes, only to realize he was struggling to breathe. He began to panic and looked around for help, but there was no one in the street; it was totally deserted. Bill lay back on the ground knowing he was going to die. The pain became less severe but his breathing was extremely hard and he could get no oxygen. Minutes passed. Then Bill saw his boss, Hamish Currie, in a van at the other end of the street. He began to crawl towards him on hands and knees. 'Get me to the hospital,' Bill struggled to say. 'I'm going to die.' Hamish laughed warily, then realizing that Bill was not joking, bundled him into the back of the van. By the time they arrived at Millport's little hospital, Bill's pain was gone and his breathing was recovered. He felt quite a fool sitting there in the van when the door was opened.

'Are you all right, Bill?'

'Yes, I'm fine. Don't bother.'

Hamish insisted on him going in at least for a check-up. Bill was taken into the examination room. The nurse asked how he was feeling and he told her what had happened. The nurse fetched Doctor Blair who, hearing the story, gave her instructions to bring the heart monitoring equipment.

Bill propped himself up on his elbow. 'D'you think I've had a heart attack or something?' he asked quite brightly expecting to be told the equipment was for something else.

'Yes, I'm afraid that's exactly what you've had.'

Bill fell back, completely shocked, and broke into a sweat. The doctor gave him an injection to sedate him.

Nan was with Leslie for lunch, and arrived home to hear the phone ringing. 'Could you come to the hospital right away, Mrs Cunningham? Your husband is here.' She was met by the nurse; Bill had had a heart attack and must be taken to the General Hospital on the mainland immediately. If she wished to go with him she must leave with him now in the ambulance.

'But my three children are just coming home from school. First I need to go and tell them what's happened. Then I'll be ready.'

Bill, regaining consciousness after the injection, heard Nan's voice. If she were to go with him, what would the children do? They would be afraid, not knowing where either of their parents were.

The doctor could not wait. The next two hours were critical. Bill could well have another attack, a more severe one and the equipment that might save him was on the mainland. There was one ferry each hour and the next was in ten minutes.

'I can't go and leave my children with them not knowing.' Nan was in tears.

'What about your friends?'

'What friends?'

The doctor beckoned her to look in the waiting room. It was packed with their Community friends. As soon as those on the farm and at the Cathedral had heard Bill had been taken to the hospital, they had put down their tools and had come straight up to the hospital to see what help was needed. Nan thought her heart would break. The love and support was there when she needed it the most. The Community would do whatever was necessary for however long it took. As Bill was lifted into the ambulance, there were his friends standing around him waving as he was driven off.

Once out of the hospital, Bill was quite determined to struggle back to health. With a young family to raise he did not have much choice. Bill Farra came to visit. The Community had been thinking about the job at the bakery and would like instead to invite Bill, Nan and the children to move up to the North College to live as part of the Community. In this way the family would have the housing they needed and Bill would not have to work strenuously in the bakery. He could work at maintenance around the Cathedral property, setting a pace to suit his health. It was hard for Bill; he wanted no one's pity if that was all it was, but eventually he said 'Yes'. In North College the Cunninghams had four bedrooms, located at the north end of the long building.

Bill and Nan sat watching television one night when for no apparent reason, Bill began to cry, really weeping. Nan was alarmed, more so when he was unable to say what was wrong. All he could find to say was that he didn't know who he was. It seemed a terrible thing to say and terrible that it was true. Bill had no knowledge of why he was saying it and no conscious feeling about it—just the tears. He wanted to get away and went out walking all night while Nan waited up for him.

Men do not cry or openly suffer pain of any sort in the culture from which Bill came. He had fought against the tears that had welled up on other occasions. A few weeks later, on a Saturday, he was walking along the sea front thinking of nothing in particular when he started crying and was unable to stop himself. He turned into a side-road to avoid being seen; he was sobbing his heart out. Seeing people in twos and threes triggered the reaction. It seemed that he was the only one who was alone—he felt desperately lonely.

Bill and Nan went to a Community Bible study group. There was an introductory time when each person was given a questionnaire, for personal consideration and reflection. The sheet of paper asked questions such as: 'What is your earliest recollection of your parents?' 'How did they encourage you?' 'What was your most creative quality as a child?' Nothing! Nothing! Bill began to answer without coherence. The next question: 'With whom was your earliest and most influential relationship?' Bill's handwriting had grown bigger and his scrawl turned to child-like block capitals—GRANDFATHER. But his grandfather had died when Bill was three; he could scarcely remember his face, and could remember nothing else about him. The tears were welling up again, and he became so embarrassed in the room full of people that he walked out, dropping the paper to the floor. He came back later and apologized for his untimely exit, but could not explain what had been happening to him.

Bill was scheduled the next day to spend a retreat in Pat's quiet room. They talked together; Pat recommended that he had a purpose in mind for the day. He responded, 'To be honest with you, I have no purpose; the day is open-ended. I'm prepared for anything and prepared for nothing.' Then he was on his own. He started crying and spent the morning in tears. There came the awareness that the great sadness was from his childhood. Without understanding, Bill decided to remember and write down incidents from his childhood. The paper got soggier and soggier, and then the pen would not work. In the afternoon Bill walked up in the hills above Millport and found himself sobbing with loneliness. He heard himself saying, 'Grandfather' and spent the rest of the afternoon calling for him, and crying with pain and sorrow.

Only later did Bill know the circumstances that had originally caused the pain of loneliness he had carried most of his life. Bill was conceived when his father was home on leave from the Army. He never saw his son for three years. Bill's grandfather initially adopted the little boy, being as a father to him.

Bill caught polio at about the age of three and spent the next fourteen months in hospital. While Bill was still in hospital, his grandfather died, but the boy was either never told or was too ill to know what happened. Yet he lost a 'father'. When he was discharged from hospital, grandfather had disappeared and Bill's father was home. Bill had never had the chance to grieve for his grandfather.

Over the months that followed his quiet day, Bill realized that what he was experiencing was a process of growing, of accepting himself and pulling down the barriers that divided him from others and kept him lonely. Previously he had blamed the Community, or his family, or even God. They were all the things that he thought had caused the pain. Now he saw beyond this. They were all points of contact that brought up the pain that he had been carrying with him all his life.

He realized that God had brought him to the island and to the Community for this very purpose: so that he could be healed. These were the most important, though the most painful years of his life.

CHAPTER ELEVEN

What Sort of Community?

Over the past several months our contact with the Scottish Episcopal Church—most particularly with five of its seven bishops—has raised again the question of our definition.

Cumbrae Report for Advisory Committee December 1978

For two years the Communities of Celebration, in Dorset and Colorado, as well as Cumbrae, had worked to write a Constitution.

In moving from the United States and away from the Church of the Redeemer, Graham Pulkingham and other members of the Community had had to determine and define their church identity. It was clear from the experience of Coventry when the Community had a national ministry apart from the local congregation of which they were members, that while having much to offer the ordinary parochial setting, the group was in a number of ways unusual. The nature of mutual commitment and the world-wide demand for their ministry meant that the Community could neither function like, nor see itself as typical of, local congregations. What other differences were there and what did these mean to the Community and the church?

When the Community lived at Yeldall Manor, the

Bishop of Oxford had referred to them as an experimental religious order. The years of becoming established in the three subsequent locations had crystalized that suggestion into a firm definition.

With the major work undertaken in Cumbrae, the Communities of Celebration drew up a Constitution. This was not a rule in the prescriptive sense, but an attempt to describe what God had done among them in their life together; the qualities of commitment, the fundamental elements of living from one financial source, the stages individuals and families should go through in becoming members. The Community was accepted as a religious order by their Bishop and the other Scottish Bishops. Each Community was responsible for establishing a relationship with a Spiritual Advisor 'who can with wisdom and impartiality give counsel and guidance to the Chapter' and a Visitor, a bishop of the Anglican or Episcopal Church, 'to serve as the guardian of the Constitution and as the guarantor to the Church at large of the Community's sound administration, stability and right to confidence.'

Having come through a number of years of pioneering, of following the Holy Spirit's lead on a previously unknown route, the members found a new sense of strength in living with the principles of the Constitution. The Constitution described the structure of the life in terms that identified the Community of Celebration with a long heritage of communities within the churches. From the traditional church's viewpoint, the Community became authenticated. At the same time, within the Communities, the Constitution summarized the developing order of life that included single people and nuclear families in a workable and meaningful way. Those members who now saw that their whole life was committed to the Communities became Chapter Members, and the element of confusion as to who was temporary and who was permanent was removed. The Chapter in each local Community was formed of those who, having made a life-long commitment, together took responsibility for the Community's life.

As the Communities of Celebration formalized their own identity with the Church, they also formalized and consolidated their relationship to one another. The Society of the Community of Celebration was also described in the Constitution and processes were defined to enable new communities to become members. So the committed friendship of Colorado, Dorset and Cumbrae Communities became apparent in the mutual commitment as Communities of Celebration. The Community in Dorset began the process of changing its name, which till then had been Post Green Community, to the Community of Celebration at Lytchett Minster.

To the members of the Community at the Cathedral the process of defining themselves seemed at times both endless and tedious. Until then it had been possible to allow the Community's vision, its reason for being and its direction of growth to be determined by the experienced members, the 'old hands' who had lived in Houston and seemed to have lived this way for ever.

The newly formed Chapter found leadership structures cumbersome and confusing. It was a critical phase for the Community, however. For a long time, to a greater or lesser extent, members had leaned on Graham and Betty's leadership, allowing them to be parent figures to the Community. The Constitution described all Chapter members as equally responsible for the life. Their struggle into a second generation of leadership was forced on them by another factor.

As the Society of the Community of Celebration was defined, Graham and Betty realized that a significant stage had been accomplished in Scotland; the group had now been defined as one of several traditional yet contemporary Christian communities. There were, however, several strands of their history that had not been clarified.

Till 1976, the Church of the Redeemer had supported the Community financially, until both they and the Community heard God speak of discontinuing this arrangement and the Community looked to being self-sufficient. Though undefined, the relationship between the Church of the Redeemer and Celebration was still very strong. It was time to go back to the United States to re-establish links with people and to re-establish ministry. In 1980 Graham and Betty and members of their household moved to Houston.

The move effected considerable change in the working life of the Community. With Mimi in Scotland and Betty in the States there was change in the music department. Mimi began to lead the choir, taking more responsibility for overall directing, when previously she had worked more with instrumentalists. The Celebration Services office began to reflect more the administrative side of the music business while the creative research and development of new material was concentrated in the Houston household. Richard and Judith left the folk group as well as the choir, and when Sandy moved to the Community of Celebration in Dorset, the folk group eventually petered out altogether.

The transition was both traumatic and strengthening. Some members felt abandoned by the Pulkinghams while at the same time recognizing that God was at work. Cathleen, struggling to understand the change, realized that if her commitment to the Community life rested with Graham and Betty, it was not healthy.

If the Community's life always had to be stimulated and built around the gifts of Graham as founder, there was an inbuilt element of insecurity. Was the Community only there because of Graham's charismatic personality? His move to the States forced the rest of the members to take up more fully the responsibility for their life and the lives of all the members.

Those who were 'left behind' began to discover a new determination. 'We grew to love each other, though we didn't have any one person who sparkled. We were committed to us, because of who we are as those whom God had called together, with all our freckles and warts, our weaknesses. We found strengths we didn't know we had, both individually and corporately, and weaknesses, that we had known intuitively were there and had been afraid they would tear us apart. We found all these were the cement that held us together.' Cathleen discovered in the change that the Community had become a people, united while individually unique, with a new depth of love for one another.

The Constitution articulated the patterns that make community life work. In the newly-formed Chapter were people who were not used to taking responsibility for the whole life of the Community. At first, all decisions were made together, an arduous process, until everyone knew they were pulling together. Trust came through working together. It became possible to set up small working parties who would report back to the Chapter, which became the governing body that established the principles.

Barbara found the change exciting. Before the defined authority of the Chapter, she had projected a 'they' who watched critically over the Community. She had felt that someone was ready to pounce if she said or did something wrong, like beginning an inappropriate song in worship. This changed. Being part of the authority left no one to be put on a pedestal for blame or adulation. The new responsibility spread into many areas of Community life. There always had been an awareness of the individual responsibility to be sensitive to the Spirit in worship, everyone being ready with a song or a prayer or scripture verse as appropriate. Now every member would be responsible for sorting out problems and making decisions in all areas of the Community's life.

Some members had a less positive reaction. Dave Porter had lived in the Community in Cumbrae for several years now. For him the Constitution felt too institutional and hard. He reeled emotionally at the shock of the Pulkingham's move to the United States. For most of his years in Scotland he had lived in North College with the Pulkinghams; Betty had taught him to cook. He had written songs that had been included on recordings. Graham was a very special friend to him; through those years he had experienced healing, acceptance and hope. How could he sort out his personal feelings from his sense of calling as he considered membership? Was he a Chapter Member? Was he a Community of Celebration member for life?

Living alone in South College, Dave found Pat Allen's friendship very helpful. She symbolized his sense of being at home on the island and in the Community. At the same time in the midst of all the changes that were happening, could the voice of God be sifted out from the many feelings?

Though the Community finally adopted the Constitution, it was still struggling to understand its evolving pattern of leadership. With such diverse emotional responses to the recent changes, the Lord provided a gift that in many ways blended the old with the new, through the theology and teaching of Dr Frank Lake.

Graham had known Frank Lake for many years. In the early days, Frank had become one of the trustees of the Community of Celebration Christian Trust. He and Graham had had a number of helpful conversations over the years. Now Frank formed a relationship with the rest of the Community. The leaders of the Community met with him and he returned for two extended visits, meeting with everyone, going through their personal histories and discovering the inner workings of the group. He reflected with them on the questions they raised.

The effectiveness of leadership, Frank taught, rested in their ability to come to terms with their own weakness. The Chapter was the Community's leadership and any ordinary life member would become part of that leadership by virtue of becoming a Chapter Member. No member leader could be on a pedestal of perfection, nor need be. It was time to accept one another completely, with strengths and weaknesses.

Frank helped the Community understand their leadership process. The intense and involved life of the Community brings out pain and pressure from a person's past. Till now individuals could only blame the Community for 'causing' them distress. But now there was a new understanding that helped both individuals and the Community. Each person could find the ability to stand in the midst of their personal pain and turmoil with the Lord present beside them to give them strength. So they received life through the stressful situations and grew to live beyond them.

For some individuals (Dave was one) time with Frank relieved some inner pressures. There was no one resident in the Community who had the experience and skill to effectively help some of the members with the inner turmoil. Several people spent time at Lingdale, near Nottingham, which was Frank's own centre. Dave had heard in the early days of the charismatic renewal of instant and miraculous healing. Now with Frank, Dave found his way onto a path that would be life-long of living with both growth and pain.

The many threads of Community life had stretched thin, with business at the bakery, the farm, and the Celebration office. The daily worship life had reached a low ebb. Frank's arrival among them brought a rediscovery of the balance between pastoral health and corporate worship. The outcome was growth and balance between these aspects of life together.

In their daily worship, the Community began to use the offices of the Prayer Book. Before prayers, there was a time of confession to share together, as a venue for working out pastoral problems on a small scale. Where necessary members were encouraged to find pastoral counselling outside the Community.

God had sent the right tools at the right time.

The first generation—the original members of the Community—had parented and loved those who had somehow missed out on such affection in their own childhood. In this setting God allowed them a second chance, which meant also going through adolescence (and other phases) again. The second generation found themselves questioning previous ideas, structures and patterns which had been necessary at the time of growing up. Many now had become parents themselves; others found themselves approaching middle age and asking if the earlier roles still served them or if these should be changed.

For the Community at Cumbrae the emergence of the Constitution and the application of Frank Lake's pastoral insights formed a powerful combination that was to have far-reaching implications. The Constitution linked them to the Church, to its history, mystery and tradition. The second generation began to discover for themselves the beauty of the church, its cycles of feasts and fasting, the healing of confession. Simultaneously, the integration of Frank's teaching with its emphasis on respecting our individual humanity, healing its wounds, loving its weaknesses and strengths brought a more compassionate, less hierarchical pastoral emphasis to the corporate life. Members became peers—each strong, each weak, each able to love because they were lovable as God had created them. Graham and Betty were no longer hero-figures to be either lived up to or criticized but a brother and sister with whom people conversed and whose experience and wisdom was valued. It was not an easy process for any of them, but in the end it proved invaluable to them all.

CHAPTER TWELVE

To Receive with Joy

LOST AND FOUND
Many items have disappeared during the Christmas and New Year's festivities:
Betty Jane—LOST—
2 pairs gloves—golden tan pigskin, black wool with leather palms, a white crochet hat and a knitting pattern for sweater
Martha Barker—LOST—
a long red coat (around the time of the jumble sale.)
The following people have each lost a pair of navy knee socks—Pat Allen, Pat Beall, Lindsey, Arabella

Community Forum Notes 2nd January 1978

Bill and Mimi moved to the house in George Street. Michelle was twenty-one months younger than her brother Graham, who by now was both healthy and lively. The kitchen in the George Street house had been refitted and better adapted for household life. The last people to move from the Thatched House in Wargrave had boxed up their household utensils, and these were now going to be used in George Street.

Mimi worked on setting up the kitchen with Ed Baggett to help her. They unpacked the boxes of chinaware to find a complete set of matching dishes and plates. As each piece was unpacked they were more delighted than ever, carefully putting them up in the cupboard. The last ones were unwrapped and put in place. Ed and Mimi looked at the dishes and looked at each other, thrilled with the joy of having matching tableware.

Mimi had grown up in a home that while not poor was always working towards things being a little better. During the years at Coventry, Yeldall Manor and North College, Mimi had enjoyed what was there: a miscellaneous collection of whatever plates were available; she had never found herself wishing for better. But how delightful it was to have this gift. She realized God was speaking to her. 'You used to think these things were important and necessary, but you haven't even missed them. When the simplest things come along you can find incredible joy. Instead of spending life wishing for what you don't have, you can see what you have in a positive light, so what you receive will bring you great joy.'

Bill and Mimi and their children never lived just as four Farras. But slowly Millport became home as they shared their family life in the household with others. The structure of the Cathedral property and the other houses the Community bought allowed for smaller groupings and households. The town was a very safe place for raising children. Bikes could be ridden without great danger, though the streets were a bit busier in the summertime. Children could run off to play without fear of crime. The anxiety for children's safety that was normally associated with mainland Britain or the United States was far away.

With young children the drawbacks of being isolated from libraries and entertainment were not insurmountable. For children who were at the secondary school in Largs, participation in evening activities involved staying the night with friends on the mainland. But to live faithfully was to work in as many ways as possible to maximize the advantages and minimize the disadvantages of where God called the family to live.

The island life had begun to affect the Community of Celebration. The constant flurry of activity was dissipated and many distractions to God's call were averted by the isolation. Living on Cumbrae seemed like a desert time. It was like a wilderness but not one in which the people were lost. The desert fathers of the fourth century viewed the wilderness as a place of meeting God in a very stark way. Cumbrae was not quite that kind of desert, but it was lacking the distractions and comforts of urban life as Mimi had known it. There was no cinema to rush off to for entertainment. On the island, nature is much closer; it makes itself known in the cold and wind and in rain and beautiful scenery.

Rick and Leslie Roberts had three boys: Luke, their eldest, and Joshua, the youngest, were both born in Scotland; Ben was born while the Roberts family was in Australia. Though the island has a small hospital, there is no maternity ward, so Luke and Josh were both born in the hospital in Greenock. After two days in the hospital there, Leslie and the new baby were driven back to the Cumbrae hospital where they stayed for a week. Rick and Leslie were both born and raised in Texas, but their three boys were thoroughly Scottish. Well... almost.

The children all went to the local playgroup, but it was when they started at school that they became really immersed in the local community. In some ways the playgroup had been like home, with Nan Cunningham working there and other Community adults helping them from time to time. It was at school that Luke discovered he was not a Scot. One day he rushed in from school and said, 'Hey Mom, hey Dad, I'm an American!' He was five years old and though he had only been to America once when he was a year old, the children at school had been quick to let Luke know he was different, not quite one of them.

Rick and Leslie discovered that Luke was not being given bad marks by the other children; they were just making sure all the categories were well defined. Besides, Rick and Leslie knew that Luke was the type that would make special efforts to be included.

Val Nobbs had had various experiences of household life, feeling at times like an appendage to the 'real' family, the nuclear family, or somehow only one of the children. Martha and Conway Barker, married the summer after the fire and now expecting their first baby, moved to the Bungalow with Val, David and Phil. Val found the new household became one family in which she could experience herself as a responsible adult member. Martha and Val were extremely good friends and perhaps it helped that Conway and Martha did not have an already strongly established family identity around which others would have to fit.

In the 1970s when community was very popular, many church groups formed households, seeing this as a form of life with great creative potential. In reality, it was often not possible to get beyond being a nuclear family with 'additional' members. The married couple were made the 'head' of the house and quite inadvertently reduced other members, especially single people, to the status of guests. For family life to work for all members, married and single, there had to be a way for all adults to be responsible for life together. The discovery and development of such a lifestyle takes time and energy on the part of all the adults. Val discovered a new depth of expression and understanding with the group that moved to the Bungalow together.

The pattern of life, how things were ordered, was decided by the household members together. There were few formal meetings; most things were decided as they chatted over the meal table together: how the money was to be spent; how the furniture was to be sorted out. In the Bungalow household there was no unwritten rule that the married couple should have the main bedroom or other privileges. They had both trust and openness toward one another in which they could give life to each other. Conway and Martha did not make decisions which were then presented to everyone else.

The Community of Celebration had always included married and single people, old and young, men and women and children. Though individuals came to the Community as products of their culture, they learned together to live in the kingdom of God. Everyone brought with them their expectations of what family life meant, expectations of friendship, marriage, romance, celibacy, singleness, parenthood. Some expectations were extremely negative, anticipating rejection and despair. Other expectations could confuse and trap people into relationships that were detrimental to health and wholeness. Openness in conversation and sharing joys and sorrows resulted in a great deal of healing for many members. The healing occurred, to a large extent, because community brings people so close to one another.

It was during the time living at the Bungalow that Val fell in love with David Stayner. David did not fall in love with Val—to him they were just good friends. It was agony to her that she could love him so much and yet he was not interested in marrying her. David wanted to remain friends as they had been. In her determination to find a good perspective on the situation Val talked occasionally to Martha and to Bill Farra.

The extreme pain, Val realized, came from a deep sense of having been rejected sometime in her early childhood. To love and yet not find that love reciprocated spoke to her of rejection and denial of herself as a person. Bill, as a good friend not involved in Val's deep emotions, was able to offer through his friendship and objectivity both acceptance and affirmation. In being at ease with Bill, Val found acceptance and affirmation of her ability to relate to men, instead of running away. There came a point when Val had to face finally the feeling of rejection that David was not going to marry her. The miracle for her was that marriage was not the be all and end all of life. If she could not marry him, so what? They could be friends anyway. Friendship survived Val's extreme emotion and she and David found time occasionally to go out together as two people who were very fond of each other, who could enjoy each other's company.

Through a whole network of friendships Val found life, giving her encouragement and hope to make sense of the inner turmoil. The feeling of death gave way to healing and growth. The quality of friendship that can develop in a close-knit group, like a household, was for many other men and women a time of healing such as Val experienced. Society causes individuals to invest most of their hopes for affirmation and affection in romance and marriage. For many men marriage is the only relationship in which they can expect to express deep feelings or be weak. To find friendships that are open and vulnerable among men and women together not only exploded the myth, but also allowed the basic human need to be loved for oneself with strengths and weaknesses to come to the surface.

For many people Christian community, with its concern for proper behaviour, gave no place for the responses that belong to every human being. It was not an easy lesson for the Community to learn: that to be a mature adult Christian involved fellowship and encouragement for one another, as well as affection. To be a Christian was not to be sexless but human with integrity, faithful to God's calling. Christians who attempted to be sexless, thinking that their faith required them to deny their own humanity, succeeded only in repressing their responses and causing themselves problems. In a healthy group of people there must be room to be human *and* Christian, to live within the kingdom of God and with integrity to love God and one another in body, mind and spirit.

In the Community love for one another was openly expressed with affection. The local townspeople, however, could not understand two men hugging affectionately, or for that matter, the affection that was displayed by all the adult members both male and female. In this culture, and particularly as portrayed in the media, such exchanges are reserved for the marriage relationship, or at best, extended to include the nuclear family. Anyone else engaging in such behaviour is suspect: they are either homosexuals or wife-swappers, or just strange.

The life of the Community had been the context for many deep and loving friendships; they could be considered 'best friends'. Most people found there were other particular people with whom they got on very well, who were easy to talk to, easy to laugh and relax with, easy to work with. There were always, too, those with whom it was hard to communicate. There were different personalities that irritated, for no other reason than personality. But love involved making friends with the attractive and the unattractive. The Community commitment to love one another was made to all the members in a reciprocal relationship that did not depend on likes and dislikes. For health, Community life depended on all sorts of people faithfully living as the family God called them to be. Val's personal turmoil and struggle resulted in her being able to love David in a friendship that was appropriate to both of them; to be able to lay aside the cultural pressure that only validates deep friendship and affection in the sexuality of the marriage relationship, to be an expression of the Community's gift in living in the kingdom of God.

CHAPTER THIRTEEN

Extraordinarily Ordinary

FROM JERRY—Please don't pinch the pen and pad by the phone!
CARS—Vehicles should not be parked anywhere in the driveway, or on the flower beds.

Community Forum Notes 25th February 1980

Though it was indeed an extraordinary 'alternative lifestyle', to those within the Community, life seemed extremely ordinary, very full, freeing and healing, while in a very good way, plain and simple. It was those outside the Community who continued to be encouraged by and drawn to this extraordinary group of people in Cumbrae.

The summer after Kevin Hackett graduated from university he and his college room mate planned to travel to Europe for about six months, three months of that in the British Isles. While at university he had read the books by Graham that told of the life of the Community of Celebration, and decided that while in Britain, he would visit the Cathedral of the Isles. Kevin's college course included music, and he planned a career in music administration, so was particularly drawn to Betty's ministry and music. He wondered if there might not be some link between his own career interest and the Community.

Kevin wrote to the Community asking to visit. There was no answer before he departed for Europe, and since he had no idea of the location of the Community in Britain, put the idea to the back of his mind.

While in Coventry, Kevin suddenly remembered that the Community of Celebration had once been resident there. He went into the Coventry Cathedral Bookshop to ask if anyone knew of their present location, but no questions were needed—Betty's book, *Mustard Seeds*, was standing on the counter.

Kevin read the book on the train during the next few days. In the fourth chapter was a reference to the North College fire and the 'Millport Fire Brigade'. Though not thinking of himself as very spiritual, Kevin became aware that God had somehow placed the book in front of him. He could not believe this was just a coincidence. Travel plans were changed and the trip to Millport, by way of Glasgow, added to the itinerary.

Catching the rickety old train to Largs, and then standing on the deck of the Cumbrae Ferry as the island grew larger before him, Kevin still found it hard to believe the course of events.

The bus was at the ferry slip and the travelling companions got off at the first stop in the town, hoping for an obvious clue to the Community's location. They went in to a small bakery shop, still carrying their backpacks, to make enquiries. The face behind the counter was familiar; Kevin recognized Margi Pulkingham from a picture on a record cover. Kevin asked where the Cathedral of the Isles was located. Margi grinned and pointed them in the right direction.

The narrow streets sloped sharply up from the shore where sailing boats were moored in the harbour. Before them, the cinder track and a wrought-iron signpost: 'to the Cathedral of the Isles'. The leaves on the overhanging trees shimmered in the wisp of a breeze. The Cathedral spire came into view, crisp against the blue sky, rising dramatically above the steeply gabled, grey slate roofs of the College buildings.

Kevin felt a growing sense of excitement and anticipation as the two men approached the Cathedral door. Kevin was convinced that the sound coming from within must be Mimi's voice; at the time she was his favourite Fisherfolk recording artist. They walked in to find Lindsey Treen, who welcomed them and took them to find Alison who arranged hospitality for the Community. Kevin's letter had been received and answered though he had not received the reply before leaving the United States. Alison made immediate arrangements for them to stay with the Roberts family.

The day was hot and sunny and the short walk through the coolness of the Cathedral and cloisters was refreshing; the pansies and wallflowers a splash of vivid colour through the cloister windows. Ruth looked up from a graphics board and smiled. The computer rattled away in another office. Someone was tinkering on a piano further down the hallway and Steven was trying to answer one phone while another line still rang ferociously. Two small boys rolled around outside on the newly mown lawn. Kevin was struck by the simplicity of the facilities of such an internationally known group.

Lindsey then invited Kevin and his friend to tea at North College. Kevin's friend remarked, 'How nice to have met Mimi Farra,' after someone had walked through the living room. Kevin had missed her completely. Minutes later, he was greeted by Betty in the hallway. Kevin was amazed that both were quite human, ordinary.

On the back of *Mustard Seeds*, Betty had written 'God gathered his people in his remarkable bond of fellowship and they laid at each other's feet their choicest treasures, their possessions, their time, their plans for the future and surrendered them all to each other for their common good together.' The impact of the visit was profound for Kevin. He discovered a place where he wanted to belong, where it seemed he could belong.

When the Cunninghams had moved to Millport, many of their friends in Glasgow were curious about their new life.

May McKeown grew up in the Gorbals, a rough area of the Glasgow slums. It was normal for families to stay near one another, living in a close. A Scottish 'close' was a group of houses and flats opening from a common entrance or alley way onto the street. The old tenement housing of Glasgow was almost entirely built this way. Grandma and Grandpa, aunts and uncles, parents and children stayed close together. There was a strong family identity and support structure. The people were in and out of one another's houses, and everyone was expected to look out for one another. When better housing became available and families moved out, most of the family support structure was dissipated.

May had been a children's nursery nurse before her own children were born. Later she found part-time work as a cashier to boost the family's earnings.

May and her husband Steven were part of the same Methodist Circuit as the Cunninghams. Steven was a local preacher. To hear their friends' plans to move to Cumbrae was a shock. Neither Steven nor May had taken particular note of the Community's presence in Scotland, but for the Cunninghams to be involved enough to move out to the island stirred their curiosity somewhat. May and Steven, with their children Christopher and Stephanie, visited the island and the Community to find out a bit more of what was happening.

In his spiritual life, Steven had experienced a growing

awareness of the Holy Spirit as a more personalized part of the Trinity. He had received the gift of tongues which was a strange and new experience. It would be good to visit the Cunningham family to share with them what God was doing as well as to understand better the Cunningham's involvement with the Community of Celebration.

While visiting the Cunninghams in Millport, the McKeown family attended worship services at the Cathedral. It was lively and people could offer themselves to God with abandon. The building filled with colour as the sun shone on the stained glass windows, lighting up the simple tracery and filling the chancel and nave with gold. The music was exciting, tinged with anticipation of meeting with God. May's heart was lifted; she was carried along with the beauty of God in the midst of the worshippers. The liturgy itself was not so different, but had openness and flexibility. Everyone was making worship happen, rather than just one or two people. The family were thrilled and came back more and more often.

Steven and May met and chatted with Howard Clark and Jerry Barker. There was special prayer for the family and the direction of their life. The McKeowns visited regularly for two years. They spent their fortnight's holiday on the island, and when possible would come for long weekends, fitting in the Thursday evening family Eucharist, the Friday night teaching, and the Sunday morning Eucharist in the Cathedral. Steven was impressed by the Community's commitment to one another and the depth of their relationships. On Thursday nights at the Eucharist and common meal, he felt himself outside the circle of fellowship, yet at the same time felt himself being drawn towards the warm centre.

But the warmth of friendship with the Community created a tension. Among the Community the McKeowns found a quality and lifestyle of which they really wanted to be a part, and yet they were happy in their own church in Glasgow. They were not looking for another place to which they might belong. On the other hand, just knowing the people at the Cathedral, talking with them, being part of their worship life and making personal friends among them, made the McKeowns raise the question of possibly joining the Community. They began to talk regularly to Bill Farra and Jerry Barker about what it would mean to be part of the Community. The same question was discussed with their friends in the church, who had mixed feelings. Would they change denominations if they moved? Friends outside the church were easier in some ways. They understood less about what such a change would mean, but were more able to reconcile the reasons for a move. Both groups encouraged Steven and May to do what they felt was best, what they felt God was saying to them.

Two years after first meeting the Community, May, Steven, Christopher and Stephanie packed up their life and belongings to join the Community on the Isle of Cumbrae.

The arrival in the Community of the McKeowns coincided with Bill and Margi Pulkingham's move to the United States to complete the education they had left unfinished some years before. Howard was taking over the bakery management, learning all he could from Jack Penders, the master baker. Since Margi had worked on confectionery, Howard was looking for someone to take her place, so asked if May would work there. She found herself saying 'yes' right away. At home, she began to wonder about the decision; she had never decorated a cake in her life. Steven was surprised that she had agreed since she was not normally one to make quick decisions. Within days of unpacking, May began at the bakery, while Steven began to work with Community administration. Sometimes when it was very busy, she started at six, working right through the day, and the job meant a lot of standing up at the bakery table. May had not worked so many hours a day since having a house and family to keep. It was hard but rewarding.

It had been twenty years since Steven had first heard God's call to ministry in the Methodist Church. He had become a local preacher, being trained and qualified to conduct worship and preach. Would this calling and these gifts be recognized and used in the Episcopal setting? That call to ministry was still on Steven's life, but he knew he was not called to become an Episcopal priest. The Lord kept bringing this into his mind, however, so he talked it over with the Chapter. Steven joined the theological studies group with the other Community members and became a lay server in the Community and Cathedral Eucharist.

Rubbing shoulders in the closeness of community brings its own growth. That depth of relationship which Steven had seen from the outside and felt drawn into resulted in personal examination. Why were a person's responses the way they were, negative or positive? How could they be pruned and matured, to be more life-giving to friends and family?

Steven met Pat at a lunchtime meeting, a Bible study about the hunger to know God. Her approach to the subject was interesting and reflected her growing sense of the contemplative. Jerry Barker was quite a close friend of Pat's and Steven grew to know Pat more through Jerry. Day by day the Community was learning with Pat, beginning to sense the very demanding nature of her calling. Steven and Pat made time to talk together before she went into her very long retreats, and he was able to appreciate this other side of the Christian faith, to understand more. He found he was able to help her with practical things, get odds and ends for her from the shops to save her going out. They became friends.

May and Steven's bedroom was close under the roof with a skylight looking out at the changeable sky. Steven knew that the wind that whistled past on stormy nights and the rain that was beating hard against the glass were clamouring even more fiercely around the Monk's Huts, Pat's home up at the Cathedral. He lay awake listening to the storm and wondering about such a calling; he could not have done it, facing not only the misunderstanding of those he loved most to do what God had said to do, but also enduring the loneliness and wrath of the elements. His respect and admiration for Pat grew, for he knew he would have given in and fallen in line with the pressures that come against a life like Pat's. Steven found compassion and reverence drawn from within him. He experienced a spiritual closeness to Pat that revealed to him the depth of Pat's faith and the personal cost of her withdrawal. Her life was a gift to Steven.

The McKeown's house was down in the town, not far from the bakery. As far as social life was concerned, the Community was not very different from their previous experience of life in Glasgow, though people had meals in one another's home more frequently. But the children found the Community adults kinder to one another and the children seemed to sort out their disagreements without fighting. Stephanie became part of the music team for the services, playing the tambourine alongside Clare. She also began to take piano lessons. There were plays and dances in the services and when someone made a mistake, everyone could laugh about it in a friendly way.

In the town, May found the Community known for its business in the bakery and only partly for its ministry. Mostly the Cathedral life was accepted as just another aspect of island life, unnoticed. There were good friendships between individuals in the town and Community that had grown up over the years. Marion Gill, who had only recently moved to the island with her husband, became a very close friend, eventually doing extra typing and office work for the Community. The Community's music leaders, through the Choral Society, made performances of the Messiah and other classical works possible on the island. There was a kind of youthfulness the Community had brought to the island, which was home to many old and retired people from the mainland. All of this was very encouraging to May.

Stanley Fox was a native of Millport and a Roman Catholic. When he left school, he had joined the merchant navy and worked as a chef on board ship. While overseas he suffered severe sunstroke, was eventually declared disabled and sent back to Millport. Stanley spent many periods in hospital. Now in middle age, he was almost permanently unemployed. He had frequently visited the old dean at the Cathedral before the days of the Community and the property was familiar to him.

Stanley used to work for the bakery part-time in the days when the Speirs family still owned it. He still came around occasionally to talk or to help. It was there that he met and became good friends with Dave Porter.

The strain of life and bouts of illness were sometimes too much for Stanley and the relatives who helped him. One stormy evening he knocked on Dave's door and asked if he could stay the night. He stayed for a few nights, until the arrangement drifted into semi-permanence, with Stanley having a room of his own in South College. Stanley could not cope with the demands of a regular job, but the people at the Cathedral did not make too many demands on him. They were, however, worried about him. Though unsure at first either how or whether to befriend Stanley, different members of the Community were drawn into a closer practical relationship with him. Some invited him to meals, and one household made their laundry facilities available to him.

An initial attitude of 'poor soul' changed to one of respect for who he was and for his relationship to God. The acceptance helped stabilize Stanley's health and he became a friend, rather than a dependent person. Although stress could lead Stanley to show considerable anxiety, he began to fit in more readily, and for a while ate all his meals in North College with Howard and Jodi Clark. The household had a regular devotional time at the table, and Stanley would pray for the people who were talked about as well as visitors to the Community.

A Roman Catholic chapel was Stanley's anchor. Though he attended prayers and services at the Cathedral, his own church was his focus. He was a deeply spiritual and faithful person, with deep compassion for others. His ministry was prayer, sometimes spending two hours a day in the Cathedral praying for others. After one time in hospital, the Lord told Stanley that in prayer for himself and others each day he would be healed. Stanley has been healed of many fears and anxieties. He was not always clear thinking or logical, but his immense faithfulness in praying for all people, friends and acquaintances had, in many ways, taught the Community of Celebration how to pray.

The Community's awareness of God was becoming broader with living on Cumbrae. The early days of Houston and of Yeldall Manor were days of excitement, of miracles and amazing events happening. Life in Scotland had deepened the Community's sense of the greatness of God. They were acutely aware of the Lord working in their lives, often in circumstances that were quite beyond their control. One day, during a time when the Community was very short of money, an envelope with two thousand pounds arrived in the morning post. The accompanying letter was from a man who had visited the Community just fifteen days after the North College fire, a visit which, due to the confusion and lack of accommodation, lasted only an hour. In that time, he explained, God completely changed his life. He had been astonished that the Community chose to praise God in the midst of such devastation, and chose to live together in such unusual circumstances. Their willingness to trust God to meet their needs, and to believe that whatever came their way came from him, sent the man away from the island with new hope and new vision. He went on to say that God had transformed his circumstances, his entire life, through seeing the Community of Celebration accepting and grateful for the life God had given them.

Maturity brought the realization that it was not helpful to expect or require God to do things in particular ways with miraculous intervention. It was not even necessary to see God's direct intervention for people to know he was God and Father of them all. Graham's eyes were healed by God's direct intervention, but his feet were healed by an operation at the hospital on the mainland. Both times Graham received the grace of God. Physical healing came to have a new perspective—no matter where or how healing occurred it was still by the grace of God.

Each person could not expect God to change everything about themselves that they did not like, or everything they did not like about someone else, just because they wanted it changed. God in his wisdom and mercy might do something to make life easier but it was not possible to convince him. God did not have to do anything out of the ordinary in order to be God, or to prove he was God.

Over the years there grew to be a deep tolerance of the differences among individuals, of likes and dislikes and personalities. Tolerance grew for different kinds of spirituality and approaches to ministry. It was not the Community's ministry to make everyone like themselves, rather to be faithful to what God had called them to do.

The beauty of Cumbrae, its isolation as well as its inescapable weather added to the sense of the majesty of God. Worship in the Cathedral carried a sense of the heritage of worship of the many saints and faithful Christians who have worshipped God together since Celtic crosses first appeared on the western isles centuries before. For fresh charismatic and excited Christians, this location brought them into the sense of God's people through the ages, the history and traditions which brought stability and order to worship and life. The third leg of the stool came into place. Where else could such an active group go to live and become inactive enough for God to introduce them to contemplation to support them, and what better place than one which had been a home of contemplative prayer for many years before they arrived?

Worship took on a new form. There had always been daily prayer; the Community had now chosen to follow the Morning Office in the Prayer Book. Each morning before work, everyone gathered together in the Lady Chapel. The short service would begin with a time of confession, and a reading from a book such as *Community and Growth* by Jean Vanier. There was opportunity to reflect on the reading, to share any concerns which had arisen, or just to sit in the comfortable silence with each other. Then the appointed leader would say, 'Lord, open our lips' and the office would begin. The service provided opportunity for open intercession and prayer, for music and spontaneous worship. The lectionery's sequence of scripture readings took them gradually through the entire Bible. As they became used to the form, the Community found both its beauty and the gift that such ordered worship could be. They discovered that they could offer faithful worship to the Lord daily, regardless of feelings, moods or circumstances. Through this, as much through its Constitution, the Community was becoming founded in the church.

CHAPTER FOURTEEN

Craig-Ard

Craig-Ard had a steady flow of guests, over 300 in number. We ask your prayers for Bob and Cathleen as they look forward to a well-deserved winter break, and for the Community as we seek to discern and establish the Lord's plans regarding Craig-Ard guest house.

Newsletter October 1982

It was some time since the Community had been given the vision of the poppy-red flower with its starry stamen. The change of direction had happened. The Fisherfolk had laid down their guitars, they had baked bread and raised children. The farm had brought them close to the seasons and the earth. The music business wound on.

The bakery continued to be arduous work, making money in the summer and losing money in the winter, though overall it made a healthy annual profit. Celebration Services (International) Ltd. processed copyrights, sorted out royalties and sifted the many songs sent from all over the world. Most of the work in music research and development had gone with Betty to the States.

The work of earning a living and keeping family life going took most of everyone's energy and even worship in the Cathedral and the weekly Thursday night Eucharist lacked something of the old charisma.

As the annual review meetings came around, questions were asked. When was the time for the flower to burst forth again from its sheltered glen and when would the roots be settled and the grain burst out to feed the baby birds? Was it time to redevelop ministry further afield?

With the Community so involved in local life, so involved in everyday work, there was no possibility of forming a new travelling Fisherfolk team. Yet the Community began to hear God speak to them of sharing the Christian life as they experienced it, with others in Scotland and further away.

The heady days of the old Fisherfolk teams, the charismatic early seventies were past. Community members had become ordinary and found that God met them in the potato fields and by the bakery ovens. They found fulfilment in living and working with their neighbours. It was clear, however, that the worship gift which the Fisherfolk ministry had brought to the Church ten years before still had a place nationally and internationally. How could there be a forum for more people to experience Fisherfolk worship 'live'?

Bob and Cathleen had for a long time been aware that they had a gift for offering hospitality. The Community began to plan for some form of conference ministry using South College but more guest space would be needed. A hotel came up for sale along the West Bay. It was excellent, but too expensive.

A smaller guest house came on the market. The harbour around which Millport is built had several bays and sandy beaches. Most of the shops were concentrated at the west end of the sea front and further east there are more guest houses and holiday homes. Craig-Ard was toward the east and just opposite 'Crocodile Rock'.

The Community bought Craig-Ard. Most houses are

built with their front steps onto the pavement. Some have a front room turned into a shop selling a miscellany of items, mostly for the tourists. Craig-Ard was set back fifty feet, with a lawn and flower borders between the house and road. The previous owners, a couple whose daughter had grown up and moved, had used very little space themselves, so the Morrises turned a back room that led off the kitchen into a family living room. Their bedrooms were on the ground floor, across the hall from the dining room and kitchen.

Though everyone had been looking for the right place for a while, there was still a flurry of activity to prepare for the first season. Bob left the bakery and together with Cathleen and others from the Community prepared it for guests. With just three weeks before opening, the Morrises moved, with almost no idea of how to run a guest house or what a guest house in Britain involved. Unexpectedly the Lord sent a helper. Sarah McGill made contact with the Community through mutual friends, and came from the Orkneys to visit. She had worked in a restaurant in Edinburgh and taught the Morrises how to set the tables British-style and what sort of food to serve in a Scottish guest house.

Next there came John Hill, whose home town was Millport. John had just completed a course in Food Technology at a college in Glasgow. His sense of humour and cooking skills helped the Morrises through the first season. John was nicknamed 'Johnny-made-a-mess' by Clare and Hannah. If anything went wrong in the kitchen, they sang out, 'Johnny-made-a-mess!' All the staff took turns at serving the guests and washing dishes, interrupting their own meals in the kitchen to get the work done. Other Community members who normally worked on maintenance of the Cathedral property helped on a washing-up rota for some of the time.

When they moved to Craig-Ard Phil had given Clare and Hannah each a rabbit. Before long it was obvious that the rabbits could not stay. The girls were heart-broken. 'We could get you a cat', suggested Bob. 'We want Solomon,' said both girls at once. Bob and Cathleen were dubious. Solomon had been in the Community for a long time. Unlike his sister, Sheba, he was a bit of a recluse, a nervous and sometimes pathetic creature. 'We'll try him,' said Bob and Cathleen without much hope. Day after day Solomon ran away. For two weeks each day after school, Clare trudged up the hill to find Solomon at the Cathedral and brought him back to Craig-Ard. 'He wants to be our cat,' she would say firmly. Finally Bob said, 'We'll try for two more weeks. After that we must let him stay at the Cathedral if that is what he wants. If he always goes back we can't keep him locked up.' At breakfast Hannah prayed that Solomon would 'want to live with us.' When Clare came home from school that day, Solomon was at Craig-Ard—he had not run away.

Bob and Cathleen had rapidly realized that they could not offer good food and service at the rate the old owners had, so prices were raised, and since the guest house had been bought as a going concern, the regular visitors returned to find considerable change.

The meaning of running a guest house with full board in the British sense began to sink in. Before becoming involved with the Community of Celebration, Cathleen had been in a convent with three hundred and fifty women so she realized some of the work involved. Financially the Morrises were unable to afford to employ additional skilled staff so did much of the work themselves. Bob and Cathleen prepared and served breakfasts for up to thirty guests, got the two girls going for the day, washed dishes and prepared lunch for everyone. No sooner was this over than work began on the evening meal, for people on holiday like substantial cooked meals. Ann Rafferty from Millport had worked for the previous owners and stayed on as a cleaner. At seventy-three she was efficient and faster than many half her age. She brought a delightful laugh and lots of common sense to a daunting task. It was hard even to find time to get to the cash-and-carry to restock the larder. Bob, as a clergyman, had been considered a great asset as the guest house always had a service in the evenings. It was busier than when Bob had been at the bakery!

There were nights when both Cathleen and Bob were totally exhausted, feeling ready to die. Cathleen would get up the next morning, aware both of being excruciatingly tired while at the same time knowing that she was doing God's will.

The first summer season was the time to find their feet, and to laugh at themselves. As Americans, Bob and Cathleen found themselves naive about the kinds of food that should be served to guest house customers. It never occurred to them that their own cosmopolitan tastes were not everyone's. They served dishes like tagliatelli, which all came back on the plates and had to be sent to the farm for the pigs. There was the lesson of cooking two dozen eggs without breaking any yolks, and learning not to take it personally when someone sent their meal back to the kitchen untouched.

One rough and tough Scot came into the kitchen smiling at Cathleen. 'Well, Lassie, who told you how to make porridge like a Scot?' She thought, at last she was beginning to belong among these people.

Community life and worship went on and many times the Morrises were unable to go, unable even to get to daily prayers. Cathleen and the children seemed always to be late for services when these conflicted with guest house mealtimes, or many times they carried on the work while

Bob went to the service on his own. Other members of the Community, walking up from the Bungalow to the Cathedral would call in and take the children with them to Community events. It was not always the same people and Cathleen struggled with whether she was doing what a responsible mother should do.

No one had estimated the effect of the guest house schedule on a family with young children. Finding a way in the busy kitchen involved careful planning.

The following season began with a great deal more know-how. Much of the non-perishable stock—masses of loo rolls, soap powder and food stuffs—for the whole season was purchased and stored away in the cupboards as the Morrises now knew how much they would need for the whole summer.

But they still were not prepared for everything. Early in the spring, the first conference was held. It was going to be well attended, with people coming from long distances. Snow fell. Craig-Ard was equipped for summer hospitality, but not for this late cold spell. The guests were freezing. It was an excellent conference anyway, promising good things for future plans for ministry through the guest house.

Then unexpectedly Hannah became very ill. At first the symptoms seemed to indicate a bad attack of the flu, but it went on for weeks. Dr Blair or Dr Wallace came each day; they did various tests but were unable to diagnose the illness. Each night the pattern was repeated; high fever, vomitting and delirium until the early hours of the morning. During the day Hannah lay on the floor, listlessly pillowing her head on Solomon. Her arms, legs and neck ached constantly and she could not walk. Hannah, slightly built anyway, rapidly lost weight. She ate very little and was unable to keep much food inside her; the doctors were baffled.

Her bedroom opposite the kitchen door was close enough for Cathleen to be able to get to Hannah quickly, but her distress was also apparent to all the guests. In the evenings she screamed with the high fever and the doctor came at night on more than one occasion.

Jane Pulkingham worked at the guest house for the summer while on vacation from Edinburgh University. Cathleen and Jane had known each other since Jane was four, the age Hannah was now. Cathleen had looked after Jane; now Jane spent lots of time caring for Hannah. This was not the work she had expected to do for the summer, but she patiently got on with cleaning up Hannah when she vomitted in her bed and comforted her. Sharing the nursing of Hannah cemented Cathleen and Jane's friendship with one another.

Hannah grew worse; the doctor had exhausted all the tests. Then Jane went to Cathleen to share her fear about Hannah's condition. If Hannah had a convulsion while Jane was alone with her, she was afraid she would not be able to cope. Jane offered to cover for whatever other work had to be done in the kitchen or around the house, so that Cathleen or Bob could stay with Hannah.

The guests were very concerned, and both they and the Community were praying for Hannah. As the other Communities, Dorset and Colorado, heard about the illness, they too prayed. Clare was seven by this time. Jane began to notice that Clare spent much of her time watching and worrying about her sister. She befriended her, giving Clare attention and making her feel special. Other members of the Community not only prayed, but helped with the chores and did what was needed on the work schedules, offering encouragement and hope.

One morning, on his day off, Dr Blair came to the back door. Hannah's illness had been going on for several months. 'We've done all we can do,' he said. He arranged for Hannah to be seen by a consultant and after a week of tests the results were that Hannah had juvenile rheumatoid arthritis. Active periods of the illness, such as Hannah had been experiencing, could last several months followed by brief remissions. Medication was necessary all the time to subdue the symptoms. Then Bob and Cathleen noticed that Hannah was unresponsive when they spoke to her. The consultant did more tests. Hannah's hearing had been damaged possibly by the high fevers or the infection.

As time passed and Hannah's illness dragged on, the Community prayed for her. Hannah's illness was in all likelihood going to recur. She might easily be ill with it for several years before she would eventually recover fully. 'Why Hannah?' Cathleen found herself praying one day. 'She's so little and she has done nothing wrong.' The Lord spoke quite simply to her, 'I don't love her any less than my own son.' Cathleen realized that God's love did not depend on circumstances. Whether things were going well or badly, he was still present with his love.

As parents, Bob and Cathleen struggled to make family life work in the midst of the guest house and discovered what they really valued in the life and built a structure in which this could be lived realistically. They were able to discover and reinforce the foundations of their family's life through the struggle.

The Morrises could no longer carry on with the work at Craig-Ard alone. One of them had to have family life and children as first priority. Bob already had the commitments involved in being the priest so they made some practical changes. Bob and Cathleen decided that on Friday nights they would take the whole evening to be together as a family, a schedule to which they held firmly. Other members of the Community led the worship service in the guest house on Fridays and served the supper. Despite the expectations of guests, Cathleen learned to say 'No' without feeling guilty.

A new season was coming. Several young people on training schemes had worked for the guest house but were not skilled for any major responsibility in management. With several successful conferences having been undertaken the new season had more planned.

Ruth offered to work the season at Craig-Ard; she loved talking with the guests and serving them. It was a good team, Bob, Ruth and Cathleen. The routines and ways of managing that Bob and Cathleen had established the previous summers were shared with Ruth. They had fun as well as working hard. Having Ruth and others from the Community among them, helping with the worship, taking care of the children, having meals together, they felt less isolated from the rest of the Community.

The third season with Craig-Ard was the most encouraging. The conference ministry had been successful, with teaching and worship on themes including children, worship, drama and peace. The guests stayed at Craig-Ard, having all their meals there and walking up the hill to South College for most conference sessions. Members of the Community joined guest speakers to lead and teach. The Community's existing worship programme was included with that of the conference so those visiting experienced not only being at the conference, but being with the Community as well. For many conference participants, the contact had been made through the travelling teams so to be part of the Community's worship was for them as important as the teaching content.

The Community's evaluation of the conference season at Craig-Ard was very positive. Conferences were an excellent way for the Community to minister to others. Many of the bakery staff would be an asset to the conferences. Was there any way to free some of them to work on conferences, to work at least part-time on ministry?

Perhaps it would be feasible financially to increase the number and size of conferences and at the same time employ outside people for the bakery? It was agreed that an expert from outside the Community would be consulted to help the Community look at the viability and future of their conference ministry.

CHAPTER FIFTEEN

To the Ends of the Earth . . .

A new expression of worship is about to spring forth, something which draws on all aspects of our life now, something integrated, relevant to our everyday life.

Community Forum Notes 7th January 1980

When Betty and Graham Pulkingham returned to the United States after eight years' residence in the British Isles, their goal was very specific: they hoped to re-establish many old friendships and make many new contacts, thereby establishing the ministry of the Society of the Community of Celebration. Through the ministry of the Woodland Park Community and its local Fisherfolk team, as well as the involvement of the Church of the Redeemer in the revitalization of the Episcopal Church's hymnal, a wide range of Celebration's experience in worship leadership, in guitar leadership, music and liturgy, and leading children was in demand. Churches wanted to learn practical skills, acquire materials and understand the theology and life experience of the Communities of Celebration. Openings came for ministry involvement with other churches, first Lutheran and then Roman Catholic. Betty and Graham found a ready audience for the Community's experience, theology and history. However, they realized that some of the skills they had left behind in Scotland would be needed in America if the demands of the church were to be met. It was not surprising that the Lord had been preparing individuals to meet those needs.

Kevin Hackett, who had visited the Cathedral of the Isles, joined Betty in Houston and began working in the Research and Development office of Celebration.

Wiley Beveridge had heard about the 'Way In' coffee house in 1972. With some college friends he caught a vision for ministry in the coffee house style. In Huntsville, Texas they formed a small community with its own singing group which occasionally visited the Church of the Redeemer. Later, in 1977, the group seemed to have fulfilled their original purpose and after a brief visit to the Community of Celebration in Colorado, most of them went to live there. Moving again, Wiley eventually joined the Pulkingham household in 1980.

Jackie Rogers had lived at the Church of the Redeemer for several years. The worship life, and the peaceful household family life spoke deeply to her and through this she heard God speak. Jackie had heard the history of how Graham and so many others had moved to England and Scotland; she had never met any of them nor heard Graham teach. Her first contact was a choir practice where she met several members of the Pulkingham household.

She and Richard Gullen had more time to get to know one another over the next few months, working together in the Youth Ministry. Richard proposed to her and she joined the large household on Altic Street.

The new household was a surprise to Jackie. As she grew to know them, while planning her wedding, Jackie experienced a depth of caring and love for one another that left her incredibly vulnerable, in some ways too vulnerable to cope with the pressures of everyday life. It was the beginning of what Jackie saw to be a healing process. There seemed to her many ways that people are healed: psychiatrists, doctors, through spiritual healing, counselling, or primal therapy. But it was the vulnerability she experienced that made it possible to receive healing, from whatever source. She was totally accepted as she was; everyone was accepted and loved, so healing became possible.

Shortly after moving into the household, work began on the recording of the album 'Rest Awhile'. Jackie worked on it with the rest of the household and other members of the Church of the Redeemer became involved in the business side of Fisherfolk life. The schedules were very demanding and seemed quite harsh. The pressure contrasted greatly with what Jackie had seen as the patience and compassion of the group's household life. She hoped that after the recording was completed, and with Richard and Graham travelling less frequently, the household would establish an easier pace of life.

While away from Houston on a trip to visit the Community of Celebration in Colorado, Graham began to experience some quite strange pains in his jaw and neck. He had been ill for the past few years. On both sides of the Atlantic doctors had tried to deal with the recurring illness. He was variously diagnosed and treated for forms of arthritis and for high blood pressure, all of undetermined causes. He had constant medication and seemed to have adverse reactions to much of what was prescribed. Often he was quite ill, yet nothing seemed to help. The pains that Graham experienced in Colorado were completely different, so strange that he decided to spend the night with friends, Bert and Joanne Womack in Denver, rather than travel further. He woke at three in the morning with more pains which were very severe; he knew something was seriously wrong. Richard woke Bert and Joanne. The family doctor was called and he immediately admitted Graham to hospital, to the cardiac unit, and scheduled him for tests in the morning. A nurse noticed his pallor and asked, 'Are you all right?' Graham responded, 'No, I feel funny', and passed out. His heart had stopped, but he was in the right place to be helped.

Graham regained consciousness with a doctor leaning over him, passing a tube into his chest, to the heart to get medication to it immediately.

'This will sting a bit, but welcome back.'

Graham spent ten days recovering. He was doing well and was due to be dismissed from the hospital when on the eleventh day, he had another angina attack, milder, but cause for concern. The doctors decided that surgery would be necessary as an angiogram revealed that of the four major arteries, one was all right, two were seventy-five per cent occluded and the fourth was ninety per cent occluded. That last one was to need a double by-pass. Everyone in the household flew from Houston to Colorado to be with Graham, singing with him and praying for him as the time for the operation approached.

The surgery was successful, but through the blood transfusion, Graham contracted hepatitis. He could undertake no work till the hepatitis was gone. For the heart surgery, a few weeks or months would have been adequate convalescence, but the hepatitis stretched it out to nearly a year. Graham had been planning a year's sabbatical, but not like this—after a heart attack. But he felt younger and healthier than he had for ten years. The doctors assured him that he could expect to live a long time yet.

Steven Plummer had known Graham and Betty most of his teenage years, and had visited 'the Redeemer' many times with his parents. Like Steven McKeown, he had been a local preacher in the Methodist Church, but felt a strong calling to the idea of community and the concept of church family that he saw at the Church of the Redeemer. Anita, a trained church organist and music teacher, had hoped, after using *Sound of Living Waters*, to be able to work with and learn from Betty Pulkingham. In 1979 they were confirmed and joined the Church of the Redeemer.

At a Tuesday night parish supper, Anita and Steven heard Bill and Mimi Farra speak on the life of the Community of Celebration at Cumbrae. They heard one of Dave Porter's songs, 'Hey, hey, it's a good morning', and the line that said 'and friend don't you know, you don't have to go, you can come here to stay' spoke deeply to them of the life that they had been seeking. Steven was finishing at university, after which they considered moving to Scotland to join the Community.

Steven and Anita were surprised and delighted when the Pulkinghams arrived from Scotland and their household was set up in Altic Street just three blocks from where the Plummers lived. It seemed an answer to prayer. Through working in the choir and through much conversation and fellowship, Steven and Anita heard the Lord speak to them of joining the Pulkinghams and the rest of the household when they moved to be with the Community of Celebration in Colorado. The household, three lorries full of their many belongings including three pianos, numerous guitars, and the Research and Development offices, moved to Colorado.

In 1982 Graham was invited to be the keynote speaker at Kanuga, a large Episcopal conference centre in North Carolina. He asked members of his household to provide worship leadership at the renewal conference. It became the catalyst to a much longer development.

Since 1977 when the old International Fisherfolk team

had set aside their travelling ministry, there had been little or no continuing contact with many interested churches all over the world. In the United States and in the United Kingdom, there had been some local Fisherfolk ministry undertaken by the three Communities, but in Australia, New Zealand and South Africa there had been no direct involvement. The invitations which Celebration regularly received were for visits of such scope and duration that none of the Communities could commit their members to travel so extensively. However, when Celebration Services had agreed to market records and books in these other parts of the world, the company had done so acknowledging the need for personal involvement at some point.

Graham had not yet recovered sufficiently to travel and minister in these faraway places, so the rest of the household began to develop a new International Fisherfolk Team. Six of the adults became the new team while Anita, Steven, Graham, and the Pulkingham's youngest child, David, stayed behind to establish their new home in the Rocky Mountains. The mixture of people was interesting as the team began to form in preparation for a visit to South Africa. Richard had finished school as early as possible and his real desire was to play rock music. Kevin had graduated in business administration and was also a trained choral musician. Wiley was a nurse and Jackie taught drama in the local middle school. Martha Pulkingham, Betty and Graham's youngest daughter was 'just a high school kid'. Betty was the only professional musician. Conway Barker, a largely self-taught clown, Bill Farra and Ruth Wieting were borrowed from the Cumbrae Community for this tour. Much later David Stayner became a regular team member, and Sandy Hardyman joined their household and team permanently after being seconded from the Dorset Community for several occasions.

While there was tremendous musical diversity among the team, these were still ordinary people, meeting together to worship; generating, being part of and leading worship. There are many ways to express worship and many forms. One crucial factor involved in leading congregations and churches in worship was the relationships of the members of the team and effectiveness in reconciling their differences. Each member of the newly formed International Fisherfolk Team came with their own preference of musical style: classical, folk, jazz. Reconciliation became part of every day's work. As they rehearsed and selected music and drama for the South African tour, they brought their gifts together and used some of everyone's talents. They found reconciliation in being able to work together while not necessarily viewing music and artistic expression in the same way.

These were not young people, looking to a leader who would tell them what to do, but adults aware of their own views and ambitions, aware of the differences between them. What they shared in common was their reconciliation, and being willing to offer that reconciliation in worship.

Fisherfolk records had enjoyed great popularity for several years in South Africa, and it was time for a personal appearance. The team decided to learn one song in an African language and chose a Zulu song 'Si ya Hamba' which means 'We are marching (in the light of God)'. The song was popular throughout the tour of conferences and concerts. Betty remembered the 1978 pre-Lambeth Conference where she and two others had led the worship. Though excellently prepared and led, the workshops on 'community' and on 'worship' drew no Third World participants. While disappointed, Betty had concluded, 'Of course. They don't need to be taught about community and worship; actually, we are the ones who need to be learning from them.' Her impression was strengthened by the time she spent among the South African black communities.

The Fisherfolk were invited as special guests to Mass at a Roman Catholic seminary. Those present prayed specifically for the tour. The celebrant was a Belgian priest and he led the most racially mixed congregation the team were to meet. There was a band playing a marimba mass setting. Mid-way through the service the rains came, thundering down on the tin roof and drowning out all speech. The local people said it was a sign of God's blessing on the Fisherfolk. There was a special sense of this being a kingdom event; the team were Anglican and the congregation were Roman Catholics; Blacks, Coloureds, Whites, Belgians, Europeans and Americans.

Richard found the visit to South Africa moving. He had expected the blacks to sing because, as Western media often portrayed them, 'they are a happy people'. White people, Richard said, associate singing and dancing with happiness. In fact the black people sing and dance through the whole of life—in joy and in pain.

For Jackie it was, indeed, as beautiful as she had been told it would be. But the racial problem that plagued South Africa was as difficult to anticipate as were her own reactions. The white people she met all had black servants who were treated with varying degrees of kindness or unkindness. It was strange to find a servant standing by to make her bed, pick up things she left, iron her clothes. Yet it seemed that to do such tasks herself was to suggest the servants were doing their work badly.

The white people lived in beauty with immaculate houses, beautiful gardens and spotless windows. The black people lived in squalor, but they were beautiful people because of their approach to life and their culture.

Some people spoke of feeling trapped by apartheid, not being able to live any other way. 'This is the way it has to be. If we start changing things individually, in our homes and our lives, in our attitudes, then that is going to affect society and we will become outcasts. South Africa,' they said, 'is a difficult place to live.' Some families were making an effort, like one family with whom Jackie stayed during the tour. They had always lived in South Africa and had accepted the culture as right and normal until they read *The Covenant* by James Michener. They became aware of the depth of oppression under which the black people lived. How might they now relate to black people? How could they begin to change aspects of their own lifestyle? There were other families who had in secret hired a man and woman, husband and wife, as gardener and cook, covering up the fact that they were married. It was illegal to have a black family living, for whatever reason, in an area specified for whites. They were supposed to live outside in the black homelands. A lot of black fathers worked in areas that kept them separate from their families for all but a few weeks of the year. White people felt the difficulty of the situation, and struggled to change what they could.

The Bishop's wife in Pretoria arranged an evening of music. There were Afrikaaners, a Zulu Roman Catholic seminary group, and several choirs from black and Anglican churches. The Zulu choir was impressive, communicating above all that life is beautiful and there is music for everything in life. The Fisherfolk were used to Western music that by comparison seemed hemmed in and prescriptive, and they found liberation in being with the choir and drank in the fellowship. One of the team's favourite songs collected in South Africa was 'Senzeni na? Sono sethu?' which is a cry of the black South African to God saying, 'What have we done? What is our sin?' and ending with a chorus of 'Amens'.

At one and the same time, the evening also pointed out the separateness of the South African tribes of English and Afrikaaners, as well as the black peoples. On the following morning one of the Anglican clergy wives phoned the Bishop's wife to thank her for the evening saying it was the first time she had heard black South Africans sing their own music.

During the months following the South Africa tour, the team polished up their presentations. Any individual coming to one of the Fisherfolk conferences would gain a lot, but most impact was made on worship in local churches when the leaders and musicians came together. Worship and music were the main themes of the conferences, yet those attending said that it was the relationships among the team that most inspired and attracted them. Again, reconciliation was the message received. Though reconciliation was never mentioned it was seen by those at the conferences and bore fruit in the team's ministry.

In Florida, the team were invited to help at a Sunday service prior to leading a week-long conference. The first person with whom they had conversation unconsciously pointed out the divisions in the church. 'The folk group gets here about nine. But I don't know when the choir arrives; they don't do much anyway in terms of worship leadership. They don't have many people; most of them joined the folk group.' The cause of division became more apparent. The organist was both easy-going and a good musician; however, she felt quite frustrated, thinking her gifts were not suited to the congregation. Then the folk group leader appeared. Apart from being the rector's wife, she was the typical folk leader, spontaneous and 'free'. Next to this charismatic personality, the organist felt thoroughly inadequate for the responsibility she held.

Yet, strangely perhaps, the folk leader felt over-awed by the professional skill of the organist. They had never found a way to talk about the division between them. The Fisherfolk team provided a forum for conversation to begin where both could offer their strengths and weaknesses to the life of the church.

The team's tour of the United States took them to the Diocese of Pittsburgh. They were invited to go to Trinity Episcopal School for Ministry, one of the newest Episcopal seminaries in the United States. They were asked to come as part of a guest lecturer series being offered between terms. The guest-mistress wrote to them saying that four of them would be staying with the seminary staff. This turned out to mean Wiley, Kevin, Jackie and Richard. Episcopal seminaries are very grand affairs, reminiscent of the English colleges of Oxford and Cambridge. There are lots of white columns, with ivy climbing over the walls. Traditionally the colleges are quite rich. The four could imagine a quite grand hospitality suite; Desmond Tutu, the President Bishop of the Episcopal Church and the Archbishop of Canterbury had all stayed there.

The drive from the airport took them through the steel towns of Pittsburgh and Kevin thought, 'How depressing. Anytime now we will come upon a gracious suburb where the college will be.' Sure enough, they came to one where the houses were set well back from the road with beautiful lawns and neat hedges. The driver, when asked, said they were about three minutes from the college. They drove over another bridge into Ambridge, which stands for American Bridge Steel Mills; it had been built more or less as a company town. Everyone there worked either for the steel mill or in a service industry, such as shopkeepers or dry-cleaners.

'Do you know much about Trinity School?' asked the driver.

None of them knew any particulars.

'Well, it is a converted Safeway supermarket.' The seminary was right in the middle of the inner city, though not very close to the main centre of Pittsburgh. The school still looked like a supermarket, though there was decorative concrete over the windows, with a cross motif in the pattern. Across the street in the parking lot a very tall and narrow building stood alone. It was two storeys and was obviously the only one remaining from a long block of terraced houses. It seemed to be slightly tilted. The ground floor was a television repair shop, open only two days of the week.

The driver spoke. 'That's the seminary hospitality suite.'

The team laughed and said, 'Sure!'

He wasn't joking.

People from the seminary had recently redecorated the rooms and were there to meet the Fisherfolk, keen to show them around. For the Fisherfolk, to be taken to this humble location brought them back to earth, putting them again in touch with how many people live each day in similar conditions. The seminary had opted not to be in an affluent suburb or part of the university in Pittsburgh, but rather to be among ordinary people and the unemployed. The people from the seminary collected day-old doughnuts and pastries from local bakeries and took them to the unemployment line each day to serve them, along with hot coffee from an urn. Trinity School for Ministry was that kind of place.

Australia was another contrast. There were strange animals and another way of life, seeming ten years behind the States culturally; male and female roles seemed very traditional. The country was expansive and remarkably different. It felt free by comparison to South Africa. There was room to breathe!

While in Australia the Fisherfolk met up with an old friend. Mike Cockayne, the Australian priest who with two lay people had been in Cumbrae for a year and had bought the first goat for the farm, led a simple parish communion. For a long time Mike had a vision of the church as the kind of community that would fit into a parish setting. On his return to Australia, he established a small community household. Alison, a retired teacher, who had also been in Cumbrae, Anne, a social worker, and Martin, an actor, lived with Mike in the rectory of the parish in Queenbian and worked in the parish. The common worship life was expressed in morning and evening prayer each day. Others from the parish were becoming more involved both in the worship life and in serving the needs of others in the neighbourhood.

The Eucharist which the Fisherfolk attended with Mike was a regular weekly service, with a baptism. Mike took the baby from her parents and walked around the church introducing her to all the other members of the family, the family into which she was being received. From the oldest to the youngest, they met the new member. It was as if he was presenting this child to God in the sight of all the people who loved her. Mike took the baby up to the altar and said a prayer before baptizing her.

At Redeemer Baptist in Sydney's western suburb, the International Fisherfolk team met other long-time friends and stayed there for two weeks. It was here that the recording 'Worship in Concert' was made with the church music group joining the live recording.

The church around the world was again inviting the Fisherfolk to lead and teach worship. The Fisherfolk had re-emerged with a stronger and more resilient ministry. The intervening years of baking and farming in the relative isolation of Cumbrae had not only firmly established the Community's life in a local church setting, but had also renewed their worship life and ministry. The Community of Celebration had a solid identity, and the Fisherfolk ministry, which was the outward expression of that life, had been transformed—emerging to offer grain to the many people who came to concerts and conferences.

CHAPTER SIXTEEN

. . . And Back Again

In the rhythms and seasons of our human life we acknowledge the joy and sorrow of the changes, the endings and the beginnings. We pray for a deepening trust in God's eternal and changeless love, knowing that he holds all the seasons of our lives in his hands.

Newsletter October 1982

Having lived for several years with the Constitution, each Community was more readily able to use it to assess its own health and welfare. Every year in January there was a meeting of the General Chapter of the Society which was made up of representatives from each community. The gathering discussed items of concern to all the Communities. In January 1983, the representatives concluded that each of the Communities needed to be founded in a manner that would enable them to develop to a second generation and beyond.

Having arrived in Community by a variety of ways, led by the Holy Spirit, the members had to decide where the Spirit was leading them now. Many Christian communities started in the 70s had now disappeared. They had been a gift for that time only. The Society of the Community of Celebration considered itself to have an ongoing life and ministry. Therefore, attention had to be given to their stability. Graham Pulkingham as Convenor of the Society spent time with each Community helping to clarify the areas in their lives where there were factors that should be corrected or strong points to be built on.

Having spent some time with the Chapter of the Colorado Community, Graham spent June 1983 with the Community of Celebration in Dorset. It was very clear that several issues had to be addressed: leadership, ownership of property, and financial instability. The situation was complicated and in need of ongoing consultation, so Graham was invited along with his household to move back to Britain for approximately a year to help the Dorset Community.

Graham's health had been a constant concern while in Colorado. The altitude made it necessary for him to either move or continue to cope with the strain on his heart. There was as yet no obvious location for the International Fisherfolk and the Pulkingham family to live permanently. So in September the household moved to Dorset to live in East Holton Farmhouse, a seventeenth-century building that had been almost derelict but was renovated by the Community. The house was in a beautiful setting, less than a mile from Poole Harbour and surrounded by woodland, fields and a wildlife sanctuary.

There were still Fisherfolk tours to be undertaken, but there was simplicity to be enjoyed and at times endured. The team required a large rehearsal space. Electric and electronic equipment had to be set up and left in position. The place should be isolated as rehearsals were loud and seemingly endless. There was an old barn about thirty yards from the house, which the Community had used for storing tents and camping equipment. The roof was a single layer of corrugated iron that had occasional leaks on rainy days. Pigeons landed on the roof and skated down the slope. On stormy days, the wind whistled through the holes and twigs rattled and brushed the rough surface. The walls were original 'wattle and daub' and crumbly.

Richard headed up an operation to make the barn usable. A platform type floor was constructed to provide a level and even surface over the original mud floor. A new ceiling was constructed, lined with a thick layer of roof insulation and the corrugated iron was sealed against the rain. A blanket was placed across the door as a curtain against the cold. Newspapers were stuffed in some of the crevices to keep our draughts.

Right in the middle were microphones, tape-recorders and instruments set up as if it was a recording studio; almost like the real thing. When the team made their next recording, they went to Arnie's Shack in Bournemouth and set up their instruments exactly as they had been in the barn (minus the pigeons!), making recording easier.

Cars were in short supply at East Holton, so bikes were used to get to the office which was a couple of miles away in the village of Lytchett Minster.

There were times during the tours when everyone was away from home, or sometimes Steven, Anita and Jackie, who had begun formal dance training, were left behind. The lawn around the house turned into a hay field when everyone was away on a summer tour in the United States.

The household began each day with Morning Prayer. The worship opened with a time of confession: sharing with one another the struggles of their Christian walk, not as a time to sort out problems, but as a means of bringing before God and one another the work of daily life. There was scripture reading, and the canticles each came round once a week. Within a month, all the psalms were included. The imagery and emotion in the psalms captured for the household the full realm of human experience and brought it before God. It was possible to bring all shades of emotion to worship: fear, pain, rejection, hope. The liturgical form was a way of saying 'God is here' and making room for him in daily life. And it said, 'the people are here' and equally made room for them. Without a strong form, worship could deteriorate into something that overemphasizes one aspect, rather than allowing the meeting of God with his people, a kingdom experience.

The quality of worship spread into daily life. There were tasks that the household undertook together with the same care and reverence as the service of morning prayer. Kevin wrote a new hymn setting and as everyone came home, they gathered around the piano and sang it together, learning the parts until everyone knew it. They had worshipped with Kevin. He had brought a gift to the body and they shared it together.

When the team had rehearsed hard all day and were tired, there was another gift of service they received. Anita or Graham would cook supper, set the table beautifully with candles and flowers. They paid great attention to the preparation—not unlike the careful preparations for a worship service at church—so all the household could come and be fed and refreshed. Life was offered to one another and people were fed both physically and spiritually.

Christmas was a very special time, with a Santa Claus and special meals. The team joined the music leadership at Lytchett Minster Parish Church for the celebration. Wiley played the flute and Anita played the organ; the others joined the choir. This was the church the household attended while they were home.

The busy nature of travelling ministry tended to make the team feel isolated from local people and from what it meant to live as their Cumbrae family did. But the melting pot of their intense life drew together gifts from other Communities as well as from their own number. They represented in a particular way the quality of life that is the heart of Celebration. Ordinary people, ordinary Christians with various talents and gifts coming together to make an offering of themselves to God. God is willing to use the talent of each member and to give them, through one another, the means and grace to offer that gift in the life of his family. Anita had never written any music before and found in the Community the encouragement and acceptance to try, and to succeed. That composition, like all the songs, dances, dramas and poems that individuals produced, expressed the life of all the Communities in Dorset, Colorado and Cumbrae.

When the Community of Celebration on Cumbrae bought Craig-Ard, they had been planning to re-establish the Community in ministry. The commercial guest house was intended to add financially to the Community and provide facilities for conferences. South College had been used for some of the conferences and could be developed further.

This approach to ministry was, at first, experimental. Having the ministry at home was helpful to family life, but also helpful as the Community was fully integrated into the Cathedral worship life. To send out travelling Fisherfolk teams on weekends would have constantly disrupted the worship at home. What better plan than to bring the ministry to Cumbrae.

The seasons that were already complete showed promise at Craig-Ard. Those who came to the conferences were richly blessed as were those from the Community who led them. People who worked at the bakery were anxious to do less baking and re-engage in ministry to share with the church at large the fruit of the life God had given them. When Bob and Cathleen left to visit relatives in the States, the report from the consultant, who was assessing their plans and resources, was just about due to be sent back.

The Community had given the consultant all their ideas for development; changes at Craig-Ard and details of South College, records of their business ventures and details of the work skills. The report came back listing the strengths and weaknesses of the potential development. The buildings at the Cathedral were very beautiful and could be a very attractive centre for conferences. Craig-Ard would be adequate as the main accommodation. The Community's worship and life together was also a great asset and the necessary foundation for such ministry. However, the report went on, there were insurmountable weaknesses in the venture. The guest house only made enough money to pay for the Morrises upkeep. It made no further profit, and the short summer season on Cumbrae precluded making more. This financial picture made it unwise to consider transferring wage-earners from other jobs to work on conferences or the guest house. In addition the guest house, like other island businesses, had to buy in bulk on the mainland, and with transport and lower retail prices, could not raise prices to cover the cost of supporting ministry. The inaccessibility of the island was a problem. To come to a weekend conference people had to catch the last ferry on Friday—by six-thirty in the winter—and the same going back on Sunday. This greatly reduced the potential catchment area to those who could leave work and be in Largs before the ferry sailed.

By the time the Morrises returned from the States, there had been lots of discussion in the Chapter. The conclusion of the report was that there was no possibility of establishing a visible conference ministry on the island. The huge investment that would be essential, the little capital that was available, the limited catchment area—all these factors made the project unworkable.

For a month the Community deliberated, praying, asking God to show them what the situation meant. How did this relate to what he had called them to do? How were they to begin ministry to the church again?

God was telling them to leave the island, move the Community of Celebration from its home on the Isle of Cumbrae. But where? To find a new location would take considerable time. The close friends and associates of the Community were the first to know. Some had sensed that a move was in the air, but all were shocked when the news was announced.

It was a time for re-assessing individual callings too. The Cunninghams had come to Millport to be with the Community. Bill had experienced a deep renewal in himself through the fellowship and worship, but heard God saying that the family should stay on the island. He was afraid to tell Nan. God had also been speaking to Nan for a while, telling her that the family were to leave the Community. She did not know how to tell Bill; it was such a drastic change. Bill Farra asked Nan and Bill if he could meet with them. The Chapter had heard God say that the Cunningham family was not going to move with the Community of Celebration when it left the island.

With their deep love for one another there was grief to bear. Some weeks and months later Bill Cunningham walked into a worship service and found how deeply God had touched him with love for the Community and for the island congregation. The Cunninghams would always belong to the family of the Community, though they would remain with their family in the Cathedral congregation.

The Lundies had moved to the island to be with the Community. Marlyn worked with children and Ian became one of the music leaders in the Cathedral and the Community, as a guitarist. Through talking with the

Community the Lundies and their children came to the same kind of conclusion as the Cunninghams, but were not sure at first that God was calling them to continue to live on the island as members of the Cathedral.

The Community began to consider possibilities for its new location. As an Episcopal foundation, they wanted to move to a diocese at the invitation of a bishop who was sympathetic with their calling and with whom they could work. Also, they wanted a location from which they could minister as well as earn their living. Their isolation had served its purpose so they would look for a more urban location in Great Britain. The other Communities were asked to join them in prayer that they would hear God about the future.

In the Society's Chapter meetings in January 1984, someone suggested that perhaps the International Travelling team that was planning to return to the United States sometime and the Cumbrae Community which was going to move somewhere in Great Britain might join together and find a common location. Each group talked over the situation and came to the conclusion that they should be together, either in the United States or in Great Britain, but together.

Various possible locations were discovered, but had major disadvantages. Either there was no airport, an essential for the travelling team, or no means to earn a living, essential for Community life.

Then Graham received a letter from Alden Hathaway, the Bishop of Pittsburgh in the United States. As a result of contact with Graham and the Fisherfolk's visit to the Diocese and Trinity, the Bishop had been considering asking for a Community of Celebration to be established there. The letter seemed to list all the kinds of factors that the Community was looking for, including a close relationship to the seminary at Ambridge. Bill Farra and

Graham Pulkingham were sent by the Community to investigate various possibilities, including Pittsburgh. When they reported back to the Community in Cumbrae and East Holton, there was much to consider. Every member had questions, reactions, responses and fears. The quiet country environment of Dorset was an extremely creative environment with a peaceful atmosphere, but to stimulate interest in social issues an urban setting would be better. Having the seminary close by would be helpful. Going back into the United States culture, with its seeming lack of awareness of the rest of the world would be a loss. Being in the city would bring access to churches, libraries and training centres, helpful in developing the Community's gifts and ministry. Re-entering American consumerism would be a challenge; God had taught Mimi a lot about being happy without luxuries. It would be harder to be faithful in Pittsburgh.

The city would be rough offering no freedom for riding bicycles and walking. The houses would be as near together as a Scottish close; May remembered how good that had been in Glasgow. The Fisherfolk team had now toured in the United Kingdom and established a relationship with many churches and individuals it would be hard to leave. Pittsburgh would give the Community a chance to live out kingdom principles among the rich and the poor of society. The theology the Community had learned through experience was to worship God when they had plenty and also when they had nothing; they would take this gospel with them. The current trend of suggesting that 'if a person was right with God they would not be poor', was not true for the Community and it would be hard to live with the apparent prevalence of that kind of word in the States.

In May of 1984 the Community of Celebration and the East Holton household decided together to move to Pittsburgh in 1985.

Together, they began to sort out all the details and to speculate on what life would be like for all of them together. The International Team began to prepare for yet another major move of all their belongings. The Cumbrae group began to think how their belongings could be packed in boxes and sent ahead. Most of the East Holton household were looking forward to living in a Community with young children and in a life that went on even when they were touring. Betty expected that she and Mimi would set up office together again. The McKeowns shared their excitement with their relatives in Glasgow and were already planning visits back to Scotland. Stephanie was excited about American music and majorettes—and especially hamburgers—in Pittsburgh.

Yet each person seemed to feel both the stress of parting with friends and family, of changing schools, of changing countries; beginning all over again would take immense effort in establishing life and ministry.

Finally a date was set—the last remaining members of the Community of Celebration would board the ferry one last time on the 17th of July 1985.

As Abraham went on his journeying from Ur of the Chaldees to the promised land, he stopped on the way and built an altar and called the place Ebenezer, meaning 'this far God has brought us'. The Community had built an altar, and offered worship and worthy offerings to God. Looking ahead they said together, 'With the Lord's help we will do it.'

Postscript

Ash Wednesday 1985

The steps from the George Street house were slippery, the wooden planks needed repairing, and the handrail was unsteady. The cinder path turned past rain-stained tree trunks toward the South College windows alight with watery sun. Winter storms had swept a litter of twigs and branches and scattered them beneath the feet of passers-by.

The Monks' Huts were awash in a sea of snowdrops, dancing courteously in the playful breeze that hurried across from Wee Cumbrae. The bank of the bowling green terrace was scattered with snowdrops and early primroses. The calling of blackbirds, thrushes and every other native warbler carried their melody over the endless song of the wind in the trees and waves breaking on the shore. High above, the cock on the Cathedral spire moved songless.

This time of penitence and fasting is loth to be interrupted by a springtime resurrection. But all creation celebrates the life of the Spirit; its season is turning Cumbrae's winter gloom to new life that looks for Easter.... but yet it is too soon.

The day was blustery and the door of the Lady Chapel difficult to shut against the wind that pushed to get inside....

Lord, open our lips.
And our mouth shall proclaim your praise.
Glory to the Father, and to the Son and to the Holy Spirit....

Bill Cunningham was at morning prayer; he had waited with a visitor in the Cathedral till Chapter Confession was over and the wrought iron gate pushed open for others to enter. He prayed for the Cathedral congregation, for those whose renewed lives had touched and felt the glory of God's presence, but whose hearts were heavy with losing those with whom they shared God's presence.

'Lord, help this little congregation to serve you faithfully, to know what we are to become, not to abandon what you have begun. Give us among us a love for one another that we may continue as your family here.'

Come down, O love divine,
Seek thou this soul of mine,
And visit it with your own ardour glowing;

'God showed me we'll always be part of the family, but we're not going to Aliquippa,' said Nan. 'No, we're to stay here. I don't know what it will be like when they're gone. I can't imagine but we'll try to keep it going. Somehow we'll keep it going.'

'Yes, we'll tell you our story. Come down to us for lunch.'

Bill continued. 'By mistake I walked in on Chapter Confession one morning, first time I'd found I could bring myself to come to prayers since.... Someone was crying. Then I knew how deeply I loved these people, how much we belong to one another, how much God has done in us and through us. I realized the depth of my own pain and grief. I cannot stay away from them.'

O, Comforter, draw near,
Within my heart appear,
And kindle it, thy holy flame bestowing.

Ian plays the guitar. 'God brought us here to be with the Community, and he's not called us to go to Aliquippa. But he's not said anything else. Maybe we'll stay here. It won't be the same. The music won't be the same, and we don't know who the priest will be, what the Bishop will do. We want to keep the music and the worship and our fellowship together. It won't feel the same and we don't know what will happen.'

Christine's dog scuffled round her feet and dropped his head upon his paws and dozed. There are snowdrops in an egg-cup on the desk. 'Elizabeth's at playgroup.... Sandy's her godmother....' Blue-eyed, round-faced Elizabeth, who has always belonged to the Cathedral family, does not know what is changing. 'Aye, it'll be quite different.... Of course, we're quite different too. We've always had the Cathedral up here on the hill, not that we came to it, mind you, but it was ours. Now we've been changed. It will not be the same again. We want to visit them.... Some folk in the town won't miss them much, but those of us who got very involved, we're not the same.'

As a child, Douglas played around the grounds and the Cathedral's cool unhurried presence was revered. He wrote little notes on scraps of paper and hid them under loose tiles in the Lady Chapel. Someone came while he was gone and wrote answering words in careful copperplate. It could not have been the dean, could it? How would anyone know what tile to search beneath for notes from scrambling boys? Great adventures were had on the acres of undergrowth between the rhodedendrons and the Monks' Huts. Not a playground but a sacred place to creep to surreptitiously. Now it was the Cathedral that drew him, worship that compelled him week by week.

'We'll go on keeping the grounds. Christine will help me. It's not going to be the same though, just us. It takes more than us to keep it like it is now. But I come up here to get away. It's peaceful here, just working the land, making the place what it should be. Aye, it's changed and we've changed. I never went to church before but now I'd never miss. Even if none of the rest ever came, I'd never miss.'

O let it freely burn,
Till earthly passions turn
To dust and ashes, in its heat consuming;

The children gathered with Cathleen as the Ash Wednesday Eucharist began. They had collected last year's palm crosses, burned them and carefully poured the ashes in a tiny earthenware bowl.

Almighty God, you have created us out of the dust of the earth. Grant that these ashes may be to us a sign of our mortality and penitence....

The line of people moved slowly and each came to stand before the earthenware bowl.

Remember that you are dust, and to dust you shall return.

The International Fisherfolk were crowded into the refectory with the Cumbrae people. Heads bowed, tears welled....

The Lord be with you.
And also with you.
Let us pray.

'Our Father in heaven (Oh, dear God, I'm tired, I'm so tired of moving....); your will be done (It *is* good to come to be with everyone before we move, but.... I want to be home somewhere, anywhere, and have a bit of rest, oh Lord....); the time of trial (Father, my belongings, everything, packed again....); deliver us (and again, a day's rehearsal, a day's travel, a day's unpacking, another day packing); for the kingdom (Father, forgive me; give me strength to go on) are yours now and for ever (just today, dear Lord, just today...). Amen.

First Sunday of Lent 1985

And let thy glorious light
Shine ever on my sight,
And clothe me round, the while my path
illuming.

The path from George Street past the Monk's Huts speaks of hallowed ground. The Holy Spirit keeps this place; he is present and was present long before the Community of Celebration, before the Community of the Transfiguration, before the hippies, before the dean. This rocky island was wrought by God's hand when time began and the Spirit brings whom he wills to rest in his presence. This is hallowed ground.

The congregation was small, at times the music faltered. A quietness settled and an early shimmer of sun shone through the stained glass saints to flicker colours on the plain white walls. Saint Polycarp, Saint Catherine, such great saints join in worship with all who have been here but, scattered now around the world, still worship. A spirit of worship, much bigger than this tiny gathering, fills the consciousness 'with all the saints and angels'.

A fluttering; high above a tortoiseshell butterfly warmed by the sun crept from its chrysalis and fluttered down on the heads of the congregation. Its newly dried wings were scarcely firm enough to hold it steady in the still cold air. Luke Roberts and his brother Ben jostled one another, leaning over the chairs to see where it settled in the central aisle. Rick beckoned them to be still. They saw it creeping around as they returned from the communion rail.

'Ever since we have been here a butterfly has appeared on the first Sunday of Lent. Whether our celebration is an early or late one, the butterfly appears. It is always a sign that this season of fasting which leads to the death on Good Friday will carry us through to Easter—the day of resurrection.'

With creation and with all the saints and angels and all the company of heaven, God is worshipped:

Holy, holy, holy Lord
God of power and might,
Heaven and earth are full of your glory,
Hosanna in the highest.

Pentecost Sunday 1985

And so the yearning strong,
With which the soul will long,
Shall far outpass the power of human
telling;

Ten minutes to go before the service and the Cathedral is filling. Lynne Burns Gourley is being baptized....

A month or so has passed since the International

Fisherfolk left to tour round Britain visiting Grimsby, Oxford, Darlington, Nottingham before catching the plane from Gatwick. Their rooms are empty.

The Bungalow was sold this week. Craig-Ard and the bakery were sold within weeks of the decision to leave. Jack Penders bought the bakery. There is a new sign outside the guest house, fresh for a new summer season. The Farras went a few weeks ago, and Graham forgot his new leather football so Barbara posted it to him. She found some things that Mimi had forgotten and packed those too.

The packers took four days to box the belongings of twenty people. 'Some people are expressing their grief; others are just packing their grief. They'll unpack it on the other side.'

'We packed some furniture, but not enough. Bill and Mimi are trying to find some before we all get there, but there's not really much money. We fitted in some wardrobes and some chests of drawers.'

'I packed all my toys but I kept two teddies and, look, Stephanie gave me her Cindy doll.'

South College is empty of all but the rubbish that's being carried away on Saturday.

As houses are sold people are moving into North College. The Annexe is littered with boxes and signs: 'These items *not* for taking to Aliquippa'; 'Items to go'; 'Steven's office'. Through the window a sign from the children's playhouse next to the coke heap reads, 'Sit long—Talk much'. They are leaving it behind. Will they make a new one in Aliquippa and will some Cumbrae children find this one and like Clare and Stephanie dream dreams in a playhouse behind the Annexe?

Pentecost—a festival of being the Church. The festival of the Cathedral of the Isles and the College of the Holy Spirit. A Eucharist celebrated one hundred and thirty-four years after the very first Eucharist here. The air is heavy with incense and expectation. The banners proclaim 'Come, Holy Spirit'. A multitude of candles light the sanctuary, bright with the red and white of vestments and spring flowers.

Ian Lundie, red shirt rejoicing as brightly as the tulips by his side, plays the guitar. This is Leslie Roberts' last Sunday to play with Ian. Simple hymns and songs flow gently, blending with the incense and the candles, till all who worship reflect the beauty of holiness, the grace of the Spirit. Rhona Gourley usually plays the piano these days; her baby is to be baptized.

The Holy Spirit gathered these people together in the presence of God: worship is their offering; sacrifice is their praise. The wind blows where it wills, dashing rain against the windows, whistling through cracks in the ancient, carved stones. The Spirit, unseen, breathes life where he wills, breaking, moulding, remaking God's people.

The Community of Celebration has lived and worshipped in the Cathedral of the Isles for ten years. They are now a different people, going as the Spirit leads them. The congregation, renewed, continues to worship at this place where the Holy Spirit makes his dwelling.

For none can guess its grace,
Till he become the place
Wherein the Holy Spirit makes his dwelling.